DATES OF IGNOMINY FOR THE MISKITO PEOPLE

- January 28, 1860 - Signing of the Treaty of Managua
- February 12, 1894 - Moskitia is invaded by the Nicaraguan army
- November 20, 1894 - Forced annexation to Nicaragua
- August 24, 1906 - Signing of the Harrison-Altamirano Treaty
- November 7, 1907 – Killing/Death of Sam Pitts (Miskito rebel hero) by the Nicaragua army
- 1981-1986 - Thousands of Miskitos are killed by the Nicaraguan government

MISKITOS

A BRIEF PROFILE OF
AN INDOMITABLE NATION

"Taplu Uplika"

Dr. Jorge J. Vasquez

Publication of **IFLE**
Instituto de Formación de Líderes Espirituales
www.liderespiritual.com

Converse, Texas

Contact: jorgevas08@yahoo.com

Unless otherwise mentioned, all biblical quotes are
taken from the New King James Version of the Bible.
American Bible Society

Printed in the United States of America

I praise and worship my Lord Jesus Christ for giving me the blessing of writing this book. He is the one who makes all things possible.

I dedicate this work to all Miskitos who do not deny

their identity and fight for their Miskito homeland.

Especially those who gave their lives seeking the

welfare and freedom of our nation.

CONTENT

INTRODUCTION
M K (Miskut Kiamka)

I am fond of history, especially the history of my people, the Miskitos. As an evangelical theologian who strongly believes in God and His Holy Word, the Bible, I oppose all kinds of injustice and therefore sin. What I am going to share in this book is precisely the injustice that the Miskito people have endured under the governments of Nicaragua and Honduras. It is a denunciation of the abuses committed by these governments. I believe that one of the great reasons why these two countries are among the poorest in the continent of America is because of the flagrant injustice of their governments. Here are some verses from the Scripture concerning the sin of injustice:

- Deuteronomy 25:16 (AMP[1]) - *For everyone who does such things, everyone who acts unjustly [without personal integrity] is utterly repulsive to the LORD your God.*
- Proverbs 14:34 (AMP) - *Righteousness [moral and spiritual integrity and virtuous character] exalts a nation, but sin is a disgrace to any people.*
- Colossians 3:25 (AMP) - *For he who does wrong will be punished for his wrongdoing, and [with God] there is no partiality [no special treatment based on a person's position in life].*

Knowing the historical brutality of the mentioned governments, it is not an exaggeration to say

---

[1] **Amplified Bible.** Copyright © 2015 by The Lockman Foundation, La Habra, CA 90631.

that the publication of this book may put my life in danger; however, as a Christian, I cannot continue to be silent; injustice must not be tolerated.

The Miskitos of Nicaragua and Honduras, although been separated by force, we form a single nation; the Miskito Nation. These governments have exploited, marginalized and impoverished us; they are only interested in our land and its resources. Since the forced annexation to these countries, the political history and public policy of both countries show solid evidence that these governments have intentionally regarded the Miskitos as second-class citizens. Perhaps they do this because deep down they know that we are actually citizens of the Miskito Kingdom.

There are many evidences that point out our precarious situation. The economic, educational, and infrastructure situation in our territory compared to the rest of both countries speak for itself. Despite the fact that the Moskitia, through its resources generates millions of dollars to the public and private sector. This is one of the reasons why there is a perennial feeling for self-determination and for the independence of the Moskitia.

The Miskito people are an indomitable tribe that fights to keep alive their identity as a nation. Despite the historical rejection of the indigenous people of the Moskitia and the imposition of the dominant culture of the country, the Miskitos and the inhabitants of the Moskitia continue in their fight to preserve their identity and self-determination that God has given them. This struggle has increased in the last forty years and many books, reports and articles have been written about it, both nationally and internationally. Unfortunately, very few of these writings have focused on our factual history, condition, and identity as a Nation.

2

The Miskito people are an indomitable people who have struggled to keep their identity as a nation alive. Despite the historical rejection of the indigenous languages of the Moskitia and the imposition of the dominant culture of the country, the Miskitos and the inhabitants of the Moskitia continue in their struggle to maintain their identity that God has given them.

Much of the writings about our nation are in reference to the Miskitos of Nicaragua. The critical analysis of these writings show bias in favor of the Nicaraguan government and prejudice against our people. Therefore, this book focuses on offering a brief history of the Moskitia of Nicaragua from the perspective of one of her children.

Miskito ethnography tends to be confusing for many, and it is to be expected. This is because many books referring to the Miskitos have been written by people who know the Miskito people by means of books and articles. In addition, there is the fact that many foreigners who have written about our history, are already prejudiced or misinformed with respect to our historical and ethnic identity.

To all this, we must add that even the oldest writings by William Dampier and the writer with the acronym "M.W.", provide information about our people through European lenses. Regarding this, it is important to recognize that they lived in an era that deemed the indigenous as savages and inferior to Europeans. However, we cannot reject their narratives, as they provide a glimpse of the Miskito nation during that time.

The purpose of this book is to offer a brief profile of the Miskito nation and at the same time an autoethnography. As a Miskito, who has researched and knows the history of my people and longs for our autonomy, I wish to share with others a brief summary of our historical identity. I also seek to provide my Miskitos brothers and sisters of this generation and posterity, factual information to help them promote and forge a solid concept of our nation. This should encourage them to continue working on the cultural, educational, linguistic, and economic advancement of our people, both, in Nicaragua and Honduras.

With this work I join the dream of many Miskitos who envision the disappearance of the border that divides the Miskito nation. It is possible that, in a few decades, if the Lord Jesus Christ does not return before, this can become true. Our vision is not unique, there are many ethnic nations in the world that seek their autonomy and independence. They were sold out or forcibly made part of a country by the intervention of foreign powers. There are many examples like that around the world; such is the case with the Kurds,[2]

---

[2] **Kurds** – They are a nation fighting to establish their own State. They have been victims of the countries that occupy their ancestral territory and the interference of European powers. The Kurds are an ancient nation with a population of around 40 million people. Their historical territory is divided between Turkey, Iran, Iraq and Syria, which is why they do not yet have their own state. Although they have been persecuted and killed, they continue to fight for their homeland. For a homeland is not a country, but a nation, a people that has self identity in the community of nations.

Tibetans,[3] Catalans,[4] Jews,[5] etc. In our case, the British and the Americans did that.

Certainly some, especially the ruling elite of Honduras and Nicaragua, are going to reject many of the assertions in this book, but I have by my side the historical evidence and the current reality of the Miskito Nation in both countries. If they were honest and moral, they would admit it, but that's a lot to ask. Their nationalism, pride, corruption, and lack of fear of God prevents them from acknowledging the injustice we have endured as a people, regardless of political ideology of their governments.

Miskut Kiamka Nani

Moihki bara laikra nani, kaisa wan Dawan Jisusra kassak lukaia, won kupia aiska wal. Yawon baha daukbia kaka, Witin wan pri laka, bara wan tasbaya ba wankbia; kuntry kum mankaia sip kabia. Kaisa Dawara

---

[3] **Tibetans** - They are a nation that has historically lived in Tibet, which is under the dominion of the Chinese Communists. Another group live in India, in the Ladakh region. Currently, there are an estimated 7.5 million Tibetans. Despite the genocide they have faced on the hands of the Chinese communist government, they do not claudicate in their struggle to have their own State.

[4] **Catalans** – They are a nation that has lived in the Iberian Peninsula; Spain, in particular. They have a population of more than 7 million. Despite the repression from the Spanish government, the Catalans continue to seek their independence.

[5] **Jews** - They are an ancient, biblical, and historical nation that had been expelled from their ancestral land by the European powers; they occupied their land and then distributed it to the Arabs (Palestinians), Druze, Circassians, etc. Today there are more than 14 million Jews, most of them living in Israel and the United States. Although around 7 million live in their ancestral homeland, still, much of their biblical territory is under the sovereignty of Jordan and Syria. Despite this, the world powers want to give the little territory they have to the Arabs (called Palestinians).

mayunaia. Miriki nikru nani, pri laka plikikantaim, witin nani pyua banira Dawanra mayunikan naha lawana wal: *We Shall Overcome (Yawon Pura Lubiasa).*

Witin nani Dawanra mayunan, aipurasunan, baku sin, gabarment mapara bui banhgwan. Gabarment puliska nani bui witin nani kum kum ikankan, wala nani silak watlara blikan, sakuna tnatara ai pri laka alkan. Yawon nani baku daukaiasa. Wan dama Ibraham Gadkaba wan Gadkasa – Witin wan prilaka wankbia.

We Shall Overcome - Yawon Pura Lubiasa - Hemos de Vencer

Lyrics derived from Charles Tindley's gospel song "I'll Overcome Some Day" (1900)

We shall overcome, we shall overcome
We shall overcome some day
Oh, deep in my heart, I do believe
We shall overcome some day

We are not afraid, we are not afraid
We are not afraid today
Oh, deep in my heart, I do believe
We are not afraid today

Yawon pura lubiasa, yawon pura lubiasa
Yu kum, yawon pura lubia sa
Kupi aiskana wal yang lukisna
Yu kum, yawon pura lubia sa

Yawon sibrin apusa, Yawon sibrin apusa,
Naiwa yawon sibrin apusa,
Kupi aiskana wal yang lukisna
Naiwa yawon sibrin apusa

1
ETHNIC IDENTITY
M K (Miskut Kiamka)

For more than a century, the governments of Nicaragua and Honduras have sought to indoctrinate the Miskitos in order to impose the dominant culture and confound the history of our people. However, the vast majority of Miskitos maintain a firm stance regarding their identity as a nation: their history, their ethnicity, their language, and their ancestral culture. As with other ethnic nations, there is a small minority that denies their Miskito roots. This is probably due to three reasons: The ignorance of our true history, the discrimination we suffer, and the indoctrination and imposition of Nicaraguan culture and history.

Personally, I have always identified myself as Miskito, whether in Nicaragua, the United States, Guatemala, Israel or any country where I visit and asked me about my roots. God wanted me to be a Miskito and that is very important to me; I thank Him for that. I am a Miskito and I tell my children that they are too.

An Undeniable Reality

Between the fifteenth and nineteenth centuries, while throughout the Americas, indian nations were killed, enslaved, their lands taken, and their treasures violently removed by European powers, pirates and settlers, an indigenous nation marked the exception. This exception was the Miskito nation. The Miskito people have stood firm in their resistance against the forces of occupation, colonization, and exploitation. History indicates that

Miskito leaders used three strategies to maintain control of their lands.

- First, they militarily opposed their enemies and potential enemies. Among them were the Spaniards, the pirates, and other indigenous nations.
- Second, they were preactive and proactive in defending their territory; they attacked other groups to keep them away from their territory in order to make known their presence and power.
- Third, they established alliances, mainly with the British and with some buccaneers.

Over the years, the Miskito leaders recognized the formidable growth of the other powers (nations), so they aptly sought and then benefited from the protection of the British (Mueller 58-59). This action was the most appropriate in light of the constant threats that indigenous nations faced from European powers and Spanish colonies in the Americas[6] at that time.

But the desire to maintain national and territorial unity had a tragic end. The Miskito people and their leaders trusted and relied too heavily on their British ally. Not realizing that the British were only interested in looking for and protecting their own interests, rather than being good and faithful ally. With the growth of American power and the proclamation of the Monroe doctrine, the British began to see their allies in the Americas as expendable; among them were the Miskitos.

For the English, the Miskito Kingdom was a negotiable territory to accomplish their hegemonic goals. That

---

[6] **In the Americas** – America is considered one continent. Spanish colonies such as, Nicaragua, Honduras, Guatemala, etc.

jeopardized the Miskito independence. The United States and the United Kingdom forged other interests for this region of the world. The desire to build an interoceanic canal through Nicaragua in the 19th century and later through Panama brought many changes that negatively affected the Miskito people. The two powers made a treaty to take care of their interests; that treaty is called Clayton-Bulwer. This treaty was used by the Americans to force the British to renounce part of certain interests of Great Britain in Central America, such as the Miskito Coast, its settlement in British Honduras (Belize) and the Bay Islands.

This action laid the groundwork for the territory and the Miskito nation (along with other ethnicities of the Moskitia) to be "necessarily" annexed to the state of Nicaragua and Honduras. This event has marked a strong and permanent repudiation of the Miskito people. After more than 100 years as part of Honduras and Nicaragua, the vast majority of the Miskitos still maintain that fighting spirit and the dream of being able to regain control of their land; to be an independent nation. As long as that vision is kept alive, there is hope. That is why the governments of both countries seek by all means to corrupt our traditions, divide our people, and seduce with and impose their culture and language on the Miskito nation and throughout our territory.

> After more than 100 years as part of Honduras and Nicaragua, the vast majority of the Miskitos still maintain that fighting spirit and the dream of being able to regain control of their land; to be an independent nation.

Discrimination and Ignorance

Many citizens, leaders, academics, and governments throughout the world and specifically Latin American, accuse the United States of being a "racist" country that discriminates against blacks, latinos, and others. But they never talk about the state-run and societal discrimination that dominate in these countries towards indigenous people. Nicaragua is one of those countries. The Miskitos, Sumos (Mayagnas), Ramas, and Creoles have experienced this. Here is an exhortation from the Lord Jesus Christ to all:

Matthew 7:3-5 (NKJV[7])

> *And why do you look at the speck in your brother's eye, but do not consider the plank in your own eye?* [4] *Or how can you say to your brother, 'Let me remove the speck from your eye'; and look, a plank is in your own eye?* [5] *Hypocrite! First remove the plank from your own eye, and then you will see clearly to remove the speck from your brother's eye.*

For example, here is a story about discrimination in Nicaragua. Although this happened many years ago, the reality has changed very little. When the Sandinistas took power in Nicaragua in July 19, 1979, they brought many terrorists and left-wing rebels; they were known as "internationalists." They were Cubans, Palestinians (from the PLO), Bulgarians, Peruvians (from Shining Path), Uruguayans (Tupamaros) etc.; we would run into them in the city buses.

---

[7] New King James Version - 1982 by Thomas Nelson. Used by permission.

It turns out that many years ago, in 1982, three of us Miskitos were on a bus in Managua.[8] There were also two brothers from the Coast, (Moskitia) of African origin (they were black). As Miskitos we were speaking in Miskito, and because of our appearance and language, and the fact that most Nicaraguans are ignorant of the Miskito culture, it seems that these traveling Nicaraguans believed we were internationalists. The point is that some of them looked at the costeños, (black men who live in the Moskitia) and said amongst: "What are these monkeys doing here, they should be on the trees." Similar derogatory expressions have been made with reference to indigenous and Afro-descendants' people. This attitude is prevalent throughout Latin America.

Many Miskitos, including myself, can testify to the contempt and discrimination we have experienced in our own land, coming from the ladinos[9]. Here are some of the discriminatory and derogatory expressions used in Nicaragua and Honduras against Miskitos (some of these expressions are also used to refer to other indigenous people).

- "Eres un indio" - "You are an indian" (indian is a derogatory term given to natives; the expression means: you are worthless or useless)
- "Eres un mosco" - "You are a mosco" (mosco is a derogatory term used to refer to a Miskito. It also means: you are just an indian, you are ignorant)
- "Indio pata rajada" - "Cracked foot indian" (you are ignorant and useless)
- "No seas indio" - "Don't be indian" (don't be stupid).

---

[8] Managua – The capital of Nicaragua
[9] Ladinos – These are Spanish speaking Nicaraguans that come to the Moskitia from the central and pacific regions of the current Nicaragua.

The paradox of all this is that when these discriminators emigrate to the United States, the first thing they do is to develop a victim attitude. They whine when they are frowned upon or discriminated against by blacks and whites in the USA. The perpetrators suddenly become the "oppressed". However, despite that experience, they continue to discriminate against the natives of their countries. The laughable thing about all

> The perpetrators suddenly feel victims, however, despite that experience, they continue to discriminate against the natives of their countries. The laughable thing about all this is that the vast majority of these people carry mostly "Indian" blood.

this is that the vast majority of these people carry high percentage of "indian" blood. Ignorance prevents them from seeing that they reject themselves; and reject God's decision. For it is God who determines our ethnicity, place of birth and death (Read Acts of the Apostles 17: 16-34).

In short, being Miskito is a reason to be mocked in Nicaragua and Honduras. Biblical, cultural and academic ignorance in both nations leads people to be hateful, pretentious, and proud. These two countries, through their governments and society in general, have discriminated against and exploited not only the Miskitos, but also all the ethnic groups that identify themselves as indigenous. Indeed, as I mentioned earlier, this discriminatory practice against indigenous people is seen throughout the Americas.

Although the vast majority of Nicaraguans and Hondurans carry mostly indigenous blood, many deny it. It is possible that this is due to low self-esteem or perhaps because of cultural ignorance or loss of ethnic identity. The reality is that many live under the spell of their former oppressors and colonizers, the Spaniards. Everything indicates that mestizos who deny their indigenous blood and exalt Spanish, suffer from Stockholm syndrome, I would say, *Hasta Colmo* (Spanish for: How can this be) syndrome.

Personally, wherever I go, be it the United States, Mexico, Israel, Guatemala, etc., I always testify of my Miskito heritage. I thank the Almighty who wanted me to be Miskito. I have this feeling despite the strong discrimination, mockery and rejection I suffered from the ladinos; in Bilwi (Puerto Cabezas).

The discrimination was so severe that my mother would often tell us not to speak Miskito. But that mother tongue is very special and I couldn't, I can't, nor shall reject it. God gave us our language and therefore we must appreciate it. Although I have been residing outside my Miskito land for many years, I thank God for giving me the blessing of being part of this people who firmly believe in *Gad*, in the God of Israel. That is why I visit my homeland whenever I can; and I hope to return to it permanently to help my people, Lord willing.

Our Name

There are many erroneous versions about the origin of the name Miskitu (Miskito). The most likely is the one that has been transmitted through our oral tradition. The elders say that the name Miskitu comes from the name of our first indigenous Chief, Miskut.[10] It is believed that

---

[10] **Miskut** – Visit
- https://www.theguardian.com/world/2007/sep/04/weather.marktran.2/19/2019.
- Matamorros, Ruth. *Una Nación más allá de las Fronteras*. WANI. P.29

this fighter came from South America (probably from the regions of Colombia and Venezuela) and settled in what is now the Moskitia of Honduras.

> The name Miskitu comes from the name of our first indigenous Chief, Miskut.

It is possible that our original name was *Tawira*, but because of *Miskut*, a courageous leader with a strong influence for many decades, we became known as Miskutus. According to our elders, our indigenous Mayagnas brothers (Sumu) were the first to call us Miskutus, making reference that we were descendants or followers of Miskut.

Conzemus (13) states that the tribal name first appeared in the writings of the pirates. He says that the English called us "Moskite" and "Moskito". Dampier uses the last term. Other erroneous versions about the origin of our name say that "Miskito" comes from a bad spelling of the English term "musket." Others say that the name originates from the fact that the Miskito territory is plagued by mosquitoes, which is common in all tropical weather. In any case, the term Miskito is recognized worldwide as the name of the indigenous majority that inhabit the Atlantic Coast of Nicaragua and Honduras.

Since many ask why so many Miskitos bear names in English, I want to offer some explanation. The alliance with the British and the relationship with them was quite cordial. There was a treatment of mutual respect. The Miskito people of that time, as was the case with almost all the indigenous tribes, were not in the habit of using personal names. In general, individuals were identified in relation to their parents and their relationship and position within the family.

As is well known, the British as Europeans, had developed the custom of giving personal names. And many Miskitos understood the benefits of it. That is why they asked the British to give them a proper name; and as expected, they gave them names in English. This is how the use of names and surnames in English among the Miskitos began. Later, with the annexation to Nicaragua, names in Spanish began to be used.

Our Origin

Some researchers who <u>have not</u> studied our history well, connect the origin of the Miskitos to the African slaves who arrived at our shores (in the mid-1600s); fleeing from his European enslavers. But historical evidence shows that before the Africans arrived on our lands, the Miskitos already existed as an indigenous nation.

According to Newson (1987), the Miskitos originated around the year 1641 as a result of a mixture between sumos and blacks. We can categorically say that his conclusion is completely wrong. Miskitos are a known to have a distinct native tribe. The written history of the Miskito people begins around 1502,[11] with the arrival in our territory of Christopher Columbus. He survived a great storm taking refuge in our territory he called, Cape Gracias a Dios.

We believe in the biblical narrative that we are all descendants of Adam and Eve (Genesis 3). Therefore, our origin goes back to very distant lands, probably in the Middle East. Because of the human rebellion in Babel (The Tower of Babel - Genesis 10), God brought confusion of language, the only language that existed

---

[11] Christopher Columbus came to the Miskito Coast on September 12, 1502, seeking refuge from a dangerous storm.

was multiplied. That required emigration by families with the same language. Likewise, there were great climatic changes that arose as a result of the great global flood. As a consequence, people had to leave the area of Mount Ararat and look for better land-dwelling.

An account attributed to the Miskitos says that we were known as *Kiribi* and that we lived near Lake Nicaragua, in the department of Rivas. It is said that we were forced to emigrate by the Nicaraos who arrived in the area near the tenth century of our era. Upon emigrating, after many clashes with other tribes (Matagalpas, Mayagnas) we ended up settling on the Caribbean Coast, under the leadership of *Waikna* and his son *Lakiatara* (Mueller 30-31). I think the narrative that at some point in our history we lived near Lake Nicaragua is an invention to connect us to Nicaragua.

The popular belief among Miskitos is that our ancestors came to South America and then traveled north and arrived in the Moskitia via the isthmus of Panama. It is also likely they may have arrived by boat, by the Atlantic Sea. The fact that historically it has been known that the Miskitos are very skilled in navigating the sea, leads us to believe in that probability. Personally, after my research, I believe that the evidence leads us to believe our ancestors came from South America, arrived in Honduras (Atlantic Coast) and from there began to expand and settle in other areas.

Historically, Miskitos have no problem with marrying people of other ethnicities; which has happened in many cases. However, the evidence shows that in general, the Miskitos are genetically,[12] historically, culturally, and linguistically an Amerindian

---

[12] Read the genetics study conducted by Azofeifa, Ruiz y Barrantes.

ethnic group, with a South American connection. Again, we believe that Miskut came from South America.

Certainly, it happens that the genetic composition of the Miskitos who have lived near the

> The evidence shows that in general, the Miskitos are genetically, historically, culturally, and linguistically an Amerindian ethnic group, with a South American connection.

Caribbean coast show genetical mixture with the African. But there are historical reasons mentioned before. This can be perceived as a rejection of the African connection, but that is not the case, the point is to emphasize that generally speaking, we are natives, or as some would call us, "Indians." In fact, many Miskitos also have European blood as well.

Certainly, the Miskito nation has experienced many ethnic blends. Therefore, for many, being a Miskito is a matter of cultural and ethnic identity rather than blood or genetics. Well, in truth, in the Americas, most of us are mestizos. But what differentiates Miskitos from other human groups is our history, land, culture, and language. Our ancestors we good at transmitting our history orally, we live in our ancestral land, we have a culture that differentiates us from others, and we have our own language that we speak as a nation. And add to that the indomitable spirit of our people.

Our Flag

The Miskito flag consists of two colors; navy blue and white. Blue symbolizes our faith in *Gad* (God in Miskito). White symbolizes our community consciousness. With it, we emphasize that communal-moral consciousness is more effective and wiser than individual or elite consciousness. The red shield or coat of arms speaks of our determination to fight and protect for our nation. It also implies the promotion of our community lifestyle, where the common good is above individual interests.

Our Social and Ethical Culture

The Miskitos are friendly people with great work and moral ethics. Referring to the Miskitos, Bishop Mueller says the following: "These Indians are by no means mentally inferior to other races. They are extremely observant and alert; they have a lot of imagination. His eyes cast an ancient fire traditionally attributed to warrior races. When men sit by the campfire, they talk about the adventures and heroism of their ancestors." (44)

Socially, the Miskito has a strong concept of his ethnic identity; this is due to a strong oral tradition. He is very religious, he is welcoming, he is hospitable, and he is opinionated. That is why he is sometimes perceived as belligerent. He is protective of his interests, his land, his family, his parents. The Miskitos fight with each other, but when outsiders attack a Miskito for defending his dignity, land or family, he expects and receives support from his fellow countrymen. These are ancestral customs.

William Dampier, a 17th-century English buccaneer, describes in his 1681 diary that as far as family life the Miskitos were monogamous. They have "a wife, with whom they live until death separates them. Young people could not marry without parental approval." In contrast, Mueller, writing more than 250 years later, mentions that some Miskitos practiced polygamy (47). Dampier says something that many Miskitos categorically reject. He said that the Miskitos were clumsy to spice food. It is possible that his weak

English taste bud did not live up to Miskito cuisine. Well, the idea that Europeans know more about the culinary arts is a matter of opinion.

The mentioned buccaneer describes Miskito social life as follows (Although his knowledge was limited to the Miskitos in the area and stayed brief, we can obtain valuable information):

> The Moskitos [sic] are, in general, very civil and friendly to the English, from whom they receive great respect, both when they are on board their ships, and on land, whether in Jamaica or elsewhere, they often come as sailors. We always please them, allowing them to go wherever they want and return to their country in any vessel with that heading they wish (Chapter 3, 1681).[13]

In another narrative, Dampier acknowledges the fishing and farming skills of the Miskitos. He describes the Miskito ability to catch fish, turtles and manatees. He also mentions that the Miskito was ingenious to launch the spear, the whiting, the harpoon, or any type of dart, being trained since his childhood. "Because children, imitating their parents, never go outside without a spear in their hands, which they throw at any object, until their use makes them masters of the art. ... They have extraordinarily good eyes, and they will see a sail in the sea farther away, and they will see something better, than we do." (Dampier 1697)

Like any human group, the Miskito presents a coin with two faces; the good and the bad, however, here

---

[13] http://www.galapagos.to/TEXTS/DAMPIER-1.php.10/14/19.

we focus on the positive aspects. All in all, it is good to mention what follows. Bishop Mueller is correct when he indicates that the Miskito tends to be relentless and vindictive when he believes that he was wronged. He is patient in waiting to take revenge. The latter is not something that pleases God. Therefore, this character is more common among those who do not know and rebel against Biblical teachings.

Mueller is also right when he asserts that Miskitos are hospitable and kind, especially when they think the person has good intentions (47). The Miskito man is expressive, and to some extent sociable, especially with those he knows. Historically, he is more open to marry or get together with people of other ethnicities, be it national or international, while the Miskitas are more selective.

The Miskito woman is a fighter and is the one who ultimately protects her children (Mueller 47). Historically, the Miskito culture is promoted by the mother and with certain fathers who emphasize Miskito patriotism. The Miskita is the holder and promoter of ancestral traditions; she is hard worker and dedicated to her family. She also stresses the use of the Miskito language and identification as Miskito. Mueller is again accurate to say that Miskito children always speak their mother's language and grow up as Miskitos (46).

The elder Miskitas are tender and evoke compassion; they promote and bring stability to the family. They are respectful, serious and quiet. Grandchildren see their grandparents as parents by extension; therefore, they are seen and treated with utmost respect and affection.

Regarding ethics and morality, Mueller states that the Miskito is honest, faithful and integral (47). Human life is highly respected, therefore, immoral behaviors such as abortion and homosexuality are not common and are strongly rejected. A sin that is observed often is envy. Instead of enjoying the prosperity of other Miskitos, many show envy and jealousy through their words.

The Miskito society focuses on a community consciousness. From that perspective, there is a strong sense of empathy and collaboration. Help among members of a community is common, especially when there is misfortune or need in a family. Within this sense of community, the concept of justice and equality is deeply rooted. This cosmovision reigns; it is promoted and permeates the Miskito society.

In general, Miskitos are friendly and have the tendency to believe in the good intentions of others. However, they are usually suspicious and doubts the good intentions of the "spaniards."[14] Historically, Nicaraguans from the pacific and central regions have given reasons not to trust them much. Many of them come to our side with an air of friendship, but end up doing things that adversely affect the Miskito people.

Most Miskitos have strong work ethics and work hard to provide for their families. However, they do not believe in wealth accumulation; the focus is on providing for the family on a daily basis. Because of this, those who do not know the Miskito culture sometimes perceive them as being lazy; but that is far from reality. What happens is that we enjoy life and nature. When

---

[14] **Spaniards** (*Ispailnani* in Miskito) – Refers to the Nicaraguans who come to our land from the Pacific and central parts of Nicaragua. It is actually a term of mockery, for the Miskitos know that they are not Spaniards, but, since they think they are superior to the Miskitos because they have an ounce of Spanish blood, they are called by that name.

they have enough sustenance and hence have nothing to do, they lie in their hammock or under a tree to rest or go fishing just for fun.

Miskitos who live in the rural communities (where the majority lives) tend to get up early, around 4 a.m. to go sowing, hunting or fishing. They are usually back home around noon. Those who live in the cities, unless they have a fixed job with office hours, do their duties and errands early, then do not waste time to rest, spend time with the family, or with the neighbor.

Love and care for nature is something that occupies a special place in the Miskito social consciousness. In general, the Miskito survives from agriculture and fishing. Therefore, he has considered the earth and the sea as allies. However, as a native, his notion and treatment of nature is very different from that of today's environmentalists or ecologists.

While Miskitos consider the ecosystem a source of life and survival, environmentalists see it and use it as an instrument to project, promote and impose their totalitarian cause; their materialistic, relativistic, totalitarian, and socialist ideology. Miskitos take nature as a gift from God, but for today's environmentalist, the protection of the environment has to do with population control and the control and manipulation of the masses or peoples. In short, Miskitos and environmentalist have a different view of nature.

For a long time, the Miskito people have practiced the concept of letting the earth rest. To cultivate, an area of forest is cut and burned, but after a few years of farming, it is stopped so that the plants and trees can grow back. This is one pf the ways the Miskito people seeks to protect the environment.

Our Language

Miskito is a Misumalpa language; it is named for the first syllables of: **Mí**skitu, **Su**mu and **Ma**taga**lpa**. According to Umaña, in past times, these languages spread throughout El Salvador, Honduras and Nicaragua. It has been determined that there is a connection between these languages. According to linguists, the Misumalpas languages are family of indigenous Chibchas and Macro Chibchas languages, which come from South America. This is not surprising, because our genetics connects us to South America and we also believe that Miskut came from there.

As Conzemius states, during the independence and existence of the Miskito Kingdom, Miskito became the "lingua franca" or dominant language of the Moskitia. Indeed, the language was known by many indigenous neighbors, up to the Isthmus of Panama (84).

Like all other languages in the world, Miskito has incorporated words from the Sumo, English and Spanish languages. This is a normal and expected consequence of cultural interaction. When a nation interacts with people of another nation that have a different language, be it as a result of immigration, domination, or occupation, the result is a linguistic mixture.

Take for example Spanish, it has incorporated many words and phrases from other languages. Many centuries ago, Spain was under Roman and Arab, domination. In addition, it received many immigrants (Phoenicians, Greeks, Carthaginians, and a significant number of Celtic immigrants), as a result, the language has integrated to its vocabulary many words from Latin, Greek, Basque, German, and Arabic.

23

Miskito is not a dialect but a language (anyone with little linguistics knowledge should know the difference). It has an alphabet, a standard applicable to grammar, phonology, semantics, and pragmatics. There are three dialects within the Miskito language: The *Wanki* (spoken by the residents of the Coco river bank), the *Tawira* (spoken by the residents of the southern part from Bismuna towards Bluefield), and the *Mam* (spoken in the Moskitia of Honduras).

For most of the 20th century, Miskito was forbidden in schools; both in Nicaragua and Honduras. Today, Miskito is a language that is being recognized worldwide. Yet, due to discrimination, ignorance of their history and low self-esteem, some Miskito parents still refuse to let their children speak Miskito. However, the vast majority speak it. Miskito leaders have an obligation to emphasize the use, teaching and spreading of our language. This means that Miskito should be taught in Moskitia schools and universities. In addition, there should be a concerted effort to publish teaching materials, books and news written in Miskito.

But the most important action to restore, cultivate and promote our language would be the creation of the *Miskito Language Academy* (Miskito Bila Kulkanka). This has to be made up of Miskitos who know their language well as well as English and/or Spanish. *Baku baman yawan sipka wan bila na kau kassak daukaia* (This is the only way we can cultivate and expand our language).

> But the most important action would be the creation of the *Miskito Language Academy* (Miskito Bila Kulkanka).

Education

During our independence, education was informal. Miskito kings were educated in different places; in the United Kingdom, in Jamaica, Belize, and in the Moskitia itself. As for ordinary people, education was at home. Parents taught their children orally about the history, beliefs and traditions of our nation. They were also taught manual labor, fishing, hunting, agriculture, and construction (housing, weapons of war, boats). When the Moravian missionaries arrived, they established many schools (elementary and secondary), some Miskitos sent their children to those schools.

When the Moskitia was forcefully annexed to Nicaragua, it took a long time for formal education to reach. Meanwhile, formal schools were continued to be established by the Moravian church and later the Roman Catholic church. The Somoza's government did little to provide access to education, especially in the rural communities. With the coming to power of the Sandinista government, a literacy campaign was undertaken on the Moskitia. This helped some, but the real purpose was to indoctrinate the people with their Marxist ideology; more so than to help them to learn to read and write. In addition, the campaign was conducted in Spanish, which many natives do not speak.

As a counterpart, MISURASATA demanded literacy in native languages and creole English, this laid the foundation for educational expansion among the Miskitos and other ethnic groups. The universities that currently exist in the Moskitia are the product of the blood shed by the Miskito rebels in the 1980s. The young Miskitos of today who have access to higher education in the Moskitia must remember that it carries as a price

Miskito blood; that it is NOT due to the benevolence of the Nicaraguan government.

The young Miskitos of today who have access to higher education in the Moskitia must remember that it carries as a price Miskito blood; that it is NOT due to the benevolence of the Nicaraguan government.

Historical Physical Profile

Although many Miskitos are mixed with other ethnicities (American, European, African, and Asian), there is still a physical profile that can be attributed to the typical Miskito. Physically, the typical Miskito is found in the communities deep within the Moskitia. The Miskito tends to be agile, averages five feet five inches, with strong limbs, brown skin, his face is flat, with high and prominent cheekbones, his nose is somewhat small, his eyes are black, his hair is black, thin and straight. Below, I offer two historical descriptions of the physical profile of the Miskito.

In 1502, Christopher Columbus on his fourth trip to America, when he reached the Miskito territory of Cabo Gracias a Dios (name he gave), described the inhabitants of the Moskitia coast as inhabited by dark-skinned people who wore golden circular medallions and lived in a great river where there was a lot of gold in the sand.

Almost two centuries later, Dampier describes similarly, he says: "They are people of medium stature, but strong members; they are dark coppery, black hair, full round faces, small black eyes and eyebrows that hang over their eyes; low fronts, short and thick noses, not high, but flat; full lips and short chins "(Dampier 31-

33; Block 73-74). The descriptions of Bishop Mueller (30-35) and Conzemius (20-21), are very similar. We can say that the profile of the typical Miskito of today is very similar to that described above.

Demography

Originally, the Miskito people were purely indigenous, but over the centuries it has become very diverse in blood; there are the pure and mixed Miskitos. The oral and written history indicates that the initial mix was with other indigenous ethnic groups, then it was with the Europeans, the Africans, and finally the Asians. This miscegenation has not diminished, since ancient times, the Miskito has been open to marry people of other ethnicities.[15]

In the coastal part of the Moskitia reside the mixed ones and far from the coast live the "pure" ones. In any case, Miskitos accept their heritage and promote their cultural values, identity and language, despite living in a markedly discriminatory society against indigenous people. It is important to note that Miskitas are the most ardent defenders of their roots; men have resumed this position after our guerrilla struggle against the Sandinistas.

The current Miskito population is around 375,000 people. It is estimated that around 275,000 reside in Nicaragua, around 80,000 in Honduras, and more than 15,000 in other countries, of which the vast majority are in the United States. The number of Miskitos is likely to be much more. However, because of discrimination and

---

[15] **Ethnicities** – I do not use "races" because there is no such thing – there is one and only race, the human race. The so-called races are inventions of evolutionists and supremacists who began by insinuating the superiority of the European or white (pinkish or pale really) ethnic groups.

ignorance, many Miskitos do not identify themselves as such. It is also the case that the census carried out by the state of Nicaragua is very poor, especially in the Miskito territory. In addition, the central government of Nicaragua (The same happens in Honduras) does not want to recognize the real number of Miskitos, because that would demand more political representation and economic investment in the Moskitia.

My Mixture

I have always considered myself Miskito. After I surrendered my heart and mind to Jesus Christ and began to study His Word, the Bible, I came to the conviction that God wanted me to be Miskito. For that reason, I accept His design with gratitude. For the Bible teaches me that being a Miskito is neither inferior nor superior to anyone. No people group or person is inferior or superior to another. Those that think otherwise are fools. Even the people of Israel, which, despite being God's chosen people, are no better than any other.

> The Bible teaches me that being a Miskito is neither inferior nor superior to anyone. No people group or person is inferior or superior to another. Those that think otherwise are fools.

To demonstrate the reality of our ethnic mix, I will share my DNA (See the following figure). The result catches my attention because it confirms much of our Miskito history, starting with the belief that Miskut came from South America. Observe the indigenous part, I have 9 percent of South American native and the rest of Central America; Miskito. My Miskito ancestors come from Wouhta, a coastal town rich in history. My grandfather, on my mother's side, had a blood connection with the Miskito King lineage. It is also evident that I have European blood, from my grandmother's side; her father was from Virginia, the United States; and his mother was originally from Germany. As for African blood, I don't have much information, yet it is explainable.

The following map displays my connection

Ethnicity Estimate

Region of the World	Percentage
Native American - Central America	40%
Native American - South America	9%
Europe - France	22%
Europe - other countries	11%
Africa - Cameron; Congo, etnia Bantu	15%
Africa - Other countries	3%

Totals	
Native American	49%
European	31%
African	18%
Jew	2%

JV Ethnicity

with Africa. By analyzing the following map of Africa, and the slave trade, I can understand why I have blood from that continent. As a native of a coastal town, there was surely a mix with the African slaves who came to our lands. The history about the slave trade from Africa, those who accidentally arrived in Central America were taken from the Cameron and Congo area; my DNA corroborates that; 15 percent is precisely from that region (see the darkest arrow).

The interesting thing is that despite the centuries that have passed and the mixture that has taken place, my blood is still mostly indigenous, Miskito (40%) and if you add the 9 percent South American

Native; I am a solid 49 percent native American. I believe my genetic mixture reflects many Miskitos today.

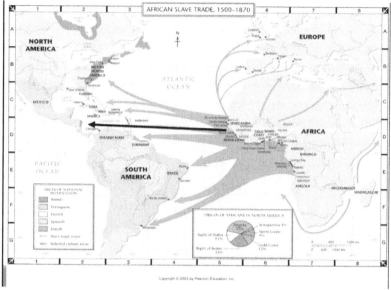

Copyright © 2003 by Pearson Education, Inc.

Our Beliefs

The Miskito is a religious person. Even before the arrival of the Moravian missionaries, the Miskito people had a high concept of the Divinity. In his diary in 1681, Esquemeling referring to our beliefs indicates that "the Miskitos believed in one God, but without any religion. Although they believed in God, they did not believe in the devil, *but they have always believed in evil spirits.* This is contrary to many Indians in America who believe and invoke him; these (Indians) do not live as distressed as those." (235 italics are mine)

  Centuries later, some writers concluded that the Miskitos had many gods; this is a speculation, for it cannot be corroborated. Usually, native tribes had idol artifacts and such, but none has been found connected to the Miskitos. We know that, in the early 1600s, some

Catholic monks had arrived and lived on the Cape for several years, they may have influenced the belief in one God ("Wan Aisa or our Father") in the region.

Offen and Rugeley affirm that between 1633 and 1635, the English Puritan minister, Samuel Key evangelized the Miskitos (13). It seems he was very successful. According to Sloane, who wrote almost at the same time as Dampier, the Miskito leaders who arrived in Jamaica during their stay could repeat with devotion the Lord's Prayer, the Creeds and the Ten Commandments (78). This is important, since these teachings were some of the ones emphasized by the Puritans. Nevertheless, it must be noted that the puritans took the son of the Miskito King to London in 1633. He may have learned these creeds while studying there.

Anthropologically it is known that the peoples of the world have had the tendency to believe in many false gods. Therefore, despite lack of evidence, it is not difficult to accept that the Miskitos believed in many gods. Add to that the influence of the Africans, who surely believed in many gods. This belief in many false gods was also real with the Europeans before the coming and the acceptance of Christianity in Europe.

There is a biblical and theological explanation for this occurrence. It has to do with the fact that human beings were created by God and bear His image, we are worshipers by nature. God created us to worship Him, consequently, if the individual or the ethnic tribe does not worship the true God, he worships false gods and images, and if not that, he worships another man, or he worships himself (as is the case with atheists).

Nevertheless, Mueller, Offen and Rugeley indicate that the Miskitos have held high regard for the belief in God, (The God of Israel) and also His Word: *Dawan Bila*, the Bible. This is very true, but lately the

31

Word of God has lost its prominence among the Miskitos due to the promotion and penetration of pagan culture and ideology.

Based on oral history, some elders teach that we

> Miskitos have held high regard for the belief in God, (The God of Israel) and also His Word: *Dawan Bila*, the Bible

are children of our father Abraham, of the Bible (Genesis 18). Miskut may have been a descendant of the ten tribes of Israel that were taken captives by the Assyrian in 722 BC ... Some researchers believe that these Israelites later dispersed throughout the world, including the American continent. This belief deserves more research.

In short, we know that the Israelites were ordained by God to be monotheists (Deuteronomy 6). However, many were disobedient to Jehovah and had many gods, which is why they were punished to be dispersed throughout the world, after many warnings (Jeremiah 32:7; Ezekiel 11:17; 36:19). Certainly, this Jewish dispersion has resulted in much ethnic mixing around the world.

To conclude this section, it is important to mention that today there are many Christian denominations in the Moskitia. This has solidified the belief in the Holy One of Israel, in Jehovah or Yahweh (*Yahwih* in Miskito). In some cases, this diversity of beliefs has resulted in conflict among Miskitos. However, the concept of being one nation that permeates the Miskito consciousness makes us see ourselves as part of a whole or an ethnic body. Let me conclude that we must also recognize that the Moravian, Catholic and other denominations have helped the Miskito people in their educational, political and professional advancement.

The Influence of the Moravian Church

The great influence that the Moravian Church has had on Miskito community life is undeniable. The Moravian mission arrived in the Moskitia around 1847; there are many positive and some negative anecdotes of their presence. Among the positive ones, we must recognize that Moravian missionaries were the ones who brought us the Gospel of Christ. Above all, it was they who made it possible for us to be the first indigenous people to have part of the Bible in our own language (According to Offen and Rugeley, 19, the first completion of *Dawan Bila*[16] was made in 1888). We will always be grateful to them for giving us that great gift. For a people or nation that does not have access to the Bible in their own language, is a people destined to lose their value in the evil grip of secularism and paganism.

The Moravian church was the first to establish educational centers in the Moskitia. Indeed, some of the last Miskito kings had their academic training in the educational centers of the Moravian mission in Bluefields. The Moravian brothers also opened primary, secondary and nursing schools and other professions. They also opened medical clinics in some of the places where they established new missions.

As for negative events, we can say that it was the Moravian missionaries who played a dark role for

---

- [16] **Miskito Bible**
  (http://worldbibles.org/language_detail/esp/miq/Miskito)
  - The first portion was published in 1889. – by the Moravians
  - The New Testament was published in 1905. – by the Moravians
  - The entire Bible was published in 1999. – by the Nicaraguan Bible Society

the Miskito Kingdom to become part of Nicaragua. The missionaries were European or American, some of them had a worldly and sinful concept of superiority and prejudice towards the natives (Miskito, Mayagna, Rama). They demonstrated this with words and actions.

The darkest role of the Moravian missionaries was regarding their attitude towards the Miskito hero Sam Pitts. The missionaries were hostile to Pitts because they opposed the Miskito rebellion against Nicaragua. Indeed, they provided support to the Nicaraguan army to persecute Pitts and other Miskito rebels. When the patriot returned from London in 1907, many Miskitos joined him again in order to fight for independence. The Miskito rebel forces led by Pitts confronted Zelaya's soldiers in October 1907. The confrontation took place between Krukira and Tuapi. Unfortunately, Pitts was wounded and died on November 7.

The support of the Moravian missionaries to Nicaragua with respect to the Moskitia, caused many Miskitos to move away from them. That resulted in the growth of the Roman Catholic church in the Moskitia. The influence of the missionaries was considerable. The Miskito pastors had little influence and vote in all of this. They did not attempt to exert power because they trusted that the missionaries were going to watch over the political, territorial, social, and spiritual well-being of the Miskito people. But that was a great mistake which has resulted in a long suffering.

Everingham and Taylor share in their investigative article about the wrongdoing of Moravian missionaries regarding the forced annexation to Nicaragua. They imply that these brothers were only focused on being able to exercise their missionary functions; free of danger to their lives and family. Instead of denouncing the injustices that were being committed, they joined it. They certainly had good intentions, but it was just that. That resulted in a Miskito Nation mired in poverty, the loss of our independence, land and dignity, the exploitation of our resources, etc.

In addition, the writings and testimonies of some of these Moravian missionaries show ethnic prejudice and nationalism. Some of them were part of the council that agreed to hand over the Miskito territory to the sovereignty of Nicaragua **(Hopefully one day the Moravian church which has its headquarters in the United States, confesses its sin and repents before God as an organization)**. For that was what their governments intended; in order to create an interoceanic canal that would pass through the Miskito territory. The interesting thing is that we currently have the same problem; but this time the interfering power is communist China. Of course, with the approval of the government of Nicaragua.

We must also recognize that Miskito Moravian pastors have played a very important role in promoting the well-being of the Miskito people. As Miskito connoisseurs of the feeling and clamoring of their people, in the nineteen sixties, they sought ways to fight to restore the dignity of the Miskito and Mayagna (Sumu) people. And also pursued the objective to get voice and vote within the structure of the ecclesial denomination. It was they who created ALPROMISU and played a key role in creating MISURASATA. It was also they who strongly supported the Miskito patriots in the eighties war. In obedience to the Word of God, they have promoted justice and rejected and denounced the injustices of the Nicaraguan and Honduran governments.

2
GOVERNMENT AND TERRITORY
M K (Miskut Kiamka)

The history of the Miskito people has been reported by prejudiced lenses. Left-wing academics have projected us as servile to the British or American empire. They claim that we were their puppets. They cannot accept the fact that we were smart enough to seek help from the British to protect our territory and people. The Moravian religious who reported our history did so from the prevailing context in that era, that we were wild and uncivilized for not living and thinking like whites. The following authors are just a few examples of the narrow-minded and prejudiced works about our nation.

- María Morelos, *Nicaragua Sandinista: Del Sueño a la Realidad* (1979-1998). A writer supportive of the Sandinistas.
- Charles R. Hale. *Resistance and Contradiction: Miskitu Indians and the Nicaraguan State, (1894-1987)*. Hale is an anthropologist of leftist ideology and therefore supporter of the Sandinistas.
- Mary W. Helms. Department of Anthropology, University of North Carolina at Greensboro, Greensboro, NC. This liberal anthropologist published many works about the Miskito people but with prejudiced. Her writings about the Miskito Nation shows superficiality; her knowledge of us was simply from books.

There are other writers that make very similar reporting and support the illegal sovereignty of the Nicaraguan and Honduran governments over our land. In fact, their writings are even more offensive, because they "paint" us as savages, uneducated and ignorant. They contend that without Nicaragua's protection we would starve to death. A similar opinion is held by many Creoles and Mestizos (Ladinos) living in the Moskitia.

The reality of our history is very different. The Miskito people love freedom, aspire to excel, are fighters, have a strong spirit of determination, are hard workers, and have a strong sense of nationhood. We like to enjoy nature. We were never slaves or puppets of any power. We continue to fight for our autonomy to forge a better future for our children. Although the government of Nicaragua; from José Santos Zelaya to Daniel Ortega have killed us and marginalized, exploited, and plunder our land, the Miskito of each generation maintains an indomitable spirit. With each passing day, the Miskito people move ten kilometers closer towards our self-determination.

Our Political System

The history of my nation teaches us that we were always governed by a monarchical system, based on a community and solidarity conscience. The Miskito King did not rule with impunity or look down on his compatriots, as used to happen with European monarchs. The Miskito King was essentially the principal among equals. For administrative and operational reasons there were distinctions of positions and functions, and these were viewed with respect. As such, the king's family was seen with respect.

Many anthropologists and historians who have written about our history argue that the idea of the monarchy was a product of the contact with Europeans. However, as Olien points out, we had a king even before coming into contact with them. Based on the Bible and oral and written history, we can categorically say that the monarchical system is not of European conception. Many peoples and tribes had it long before the European nations.

The Bible informs us beginning in chapter 11 of the Book of Genesis that all ethnic groups in the world descend from one of the three sons of Noah (Cam, Shem and Japheth). The biblical story tells us that God commanded the human race to multiply and populate the earth (Genesis 1:28 and 9:1). That order requires emigration and immigration. After the global flood (Genesis 6-8) when every living being on earth was killed, God reaffirmed his order and original intention to populate the entire earth with humans. The children of the sons of Noah rebelled against this order and prepared to stay in the land of Sinar, specifically in Babel. To that end they organized and began to build what is known as the Tower of Babel (Genesis 11). When they were in that effort, God confused the only language that existed to disperse them across the globe. The Bible also tells us that these descendants of Noah had already conceived the concept of monarchy.

With all of the above I am saying that it was not the Europeans who conceived such a system of government. The Miskitos, as descendants of one of Noah's sons, obviously continued with that system; before being influenced by the colonizers.

In the days of the Miskito Kingdom, the government was led by a king. He had a council of elders and had regional leaders called Generals, Governors and

Admirals. Olien attest that there were also captains, who were below the aforementioned leaders. He and other anthropologists and historians asseverate that Miskito society was highly structured; including a very defined political structure (See the following figure).

GOVERNMENT STRUCTURE OF THE MISKITO KINGDOM
(XVIII y XIX Centuries)

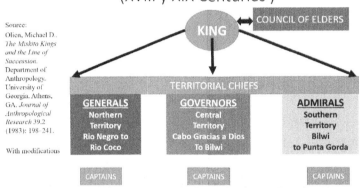

Source:
Olien, Michael D..
*The Miskito Kings
and the Line of
Succession.*
Department of
Anthropology.
University of
Georgia. Athens,
GA. *Journal of
Anthropological
Research* 39.2
(1983): 198–241.

With modifications

Before the 1750's the king had absolute control over the Moskitia. But that control declined due to the resistance of some leaders. They contended that the Miskito Sambos (Miskitos mixed with African) were exerting tremendous influence over the king. As a consequence, power was divided between three leaders and the king (he had more authority than the other three). These officers helped the king to govern the Miskito Kingdom.

As part of this community-monarchy, the king was responsible for overseeing the common good, leading the Miskito community and its military force, and serving as the maximum representative of the Miskito Nation. It is important to emphasize this concept of community, because in the Miskito mindset, the destiny of the nation must be decided by the community and not by a person or an elite disconnected from the community. That is why, as of today, the Miskito Council of Elders and pastors have such a great influence on Miskito community life.

Since the forced annexation to Nicaragua, the traditional leaders recognized by the Miskito people are:
- The Council of Elders,
- The judges or wihtas of the communities,
- Pastors, and
- Teachers.

These are the ones that influence the Miskitos and are held responsible for the situation of the community and nation. It is important to note that, with the annexation to Nicaragua, the Miskito communities have a communal leader called Síndico (Trustee); which was devised and established by the government of Nicaragua. Through this officer, the government exercises control and maintains its influence over the communities. Recently, in the last twenty years, the Nicaraguan government has used the political parties and Miskito leaders of those parties to reduce the influence of the Council of Elders, the wihtas and the pastors. The perks that these leaders receive, make them willing to take action against their own people.

Kings of the Moskitia

As mentioned earlier, the Miskito Kingdom practiced a monarchical system of government. This monarchy ran in the family and was relatively stable. Olien, Fallon and other researchers state that the Miskito monarchy was dominated by a single family for more than two hundred and forty years. With this, it is very important to draw attention to the fact that Miskito sovereignty over its territory precedes that of Nicaragua for couple of centuries. History reveals that when the Moskitia was independent, Nicaragua was just a Spanish colony.

It is very important to draw attention to the fact that Miskito sovereignty over its territory precedes that of Nicaragua for couple of centuries. History reveals that when the Moskitia was independent, Nicaragua was just a Spanish colony.

Historical documents show that an authentic Miskito king ruled the Moskitia since the 1600's, until the territory was forcibly annexed to Nicaragua. Olien correctly asserts that "while many native kings of Mesoamerica were losing their authority and control of their territories as a result of the Spanish conquest, a new political structure emerged on the east coast of Nicaragua, which became known as the Miskito Kingdom. Many writers have suggested that this political entity was intentionally created by the English. This is not the case. "(198)

Olien continues, "the structure of the Miskito Kingdom remained remarkably stable for a period of approximately 240 years (199). Fallon states the same:

> Showing a remarkable political continuity, which rivaled many of the Royal Houses of Europe, the Miskito Kingdom was in the hands of a single family for the last 239 years of the state's existence. The kingdom was a stable and successful indigenous country in a region often convulsed by Spanish colonial political turmoil. In 1638, London officially recognized the Miskito Kingdom as a sovereign state and in 1710, it concluded an official treaty of friendship and alliance establishing a protectorate over the country that would last for almost two centuries. (2019)

41

The above declarations cannot be said of any other country, tribe or kingdom in Mesoamerica. Take for example Nicaragua itself. From 1520 when Gil González Dávila began to colonize the historical part called Nicaragua (The Pacific and Center) until April 30, 1838 when it became independent, the country was plunged into political, structural and territorial chaos. We can clearly see that Nicaragua did not even exist as a country when the Miskito Kingdom was an independent territory recognized by England and even by Spain.

From: Popular Science Monthly Volume 45, page 165 - (1894). FIG. 3. The Mosquito Chief and Executive Council: (1) Robert Henry Clarence, chief; (2) Hon. Charles Patterson, vice president and guardian; (3) Hon. J. W. Cuthbert, attorney general and secretary to the chief ; (4) Mr. J. W. Cuthbert, Jr. government secretary; (5) Mr. George Raymond, councilman and headman; (6) Mr. Edward McCrea, councilman and headman. Note that all but the two Black men are obvious Mulattoes

Robert Henry Clarence (in the middle of the photo - young man with sword) was the last Miskito King. When Bluefields, the capital of the Kingdom at that time, was invaded by the Nicaraguan army, he was forced into exile in Jamaica, where he died during a medical operation.

42

MISKITO KINGS		
NAME OF THE KING	DATE OF HIS REIGN	PLACE OF RESIDENCE
Dama - Oldman	1625 - 1641	Cabo Gracias a Dios
Dama II - Luhpia - Oldman Son	1641 - 1655	Cabo Gracias a Dios
Dama III - Oldman III	1655 - 1686	Cabo Gracias a Dios
Jeremy I	1687 - 1720	Sandy Bay
Jeremy II	1720 - 1729	Sandy Bay
Peter	1729 - 1739	Sandy Bay
Edward	1739 - 1755	Sandy Bay
George I	1755 - 1776	Sandy Bay
George II	1777 - 1800	Sandy Bay
Stephen	1801-1816	Sandy Bay
George Frederic	1816 - 1824	Cabo Gracias a Dios
Robert Charles Frederic	1824 - 1844	Cabo Gracias a Dios
George Augustus Frederic	1845 - 1864	Bluefields
William Henry Clarence	1865 - 1879	Bluefields
George William Hendy	1879 - 1888	Bluefields
Andrew Hendy	1888 - 1889	Bluefields
Jonathan Charles Frederick	1889 - 1890	Bluefields
Robert Henry Clarence	1891 - 1894	Bluefields

Note: All the kings belonged to one family

Sources:

Olien, Michael D. *The Miskito Kings and the Line of Succession.* Department of Anthropology, University of Georgia, Athens, GA. *Journal of Anthropological Research* 39.2 (1983): 198–241.

Helms W. Mary. *Of Kings and Contexts: Ethnohistorical Interpretations of Miskito   Political Structure and Function, American Ethnologist*, 13, 3, (506-523), (2009).

Our Territory

As Olien attests, the Miskito Kingdom was under the command of its king, it remained independent throughout the period of the formation of what was the Federal Republic of Central America (Federation of Central American Republics) and its subsequent dissolution and independence of the member countries.

The territorial limits of the Moskitia were immense. Fallon confirms this, he says:

> "The Miskito Kingdom, an independent indigenous state, existed for over 250 years. The country was immense, occupying approximately one third of Central America. From the Caribbean coast, it extended north to include the eastern region of Honduras, south to the border with Costa Rica and west to include the central highlands. It included 60 percent of current Nicaragua. The territorial size of the Miskito Kingdom was recognized on a Spanish map of 1780, the 1840 map of Central America by Heinrich Berghaus, and the American maps of 1850." (2019) (See the following map).

> "The country was immense, occupying approximately one third of Central America. From the Caribbean coast, it extended north to include the eastern region of Honduras, south to the border with Costa Rica and west to include the central highlands. It included 60 percent of current Nicaragua"

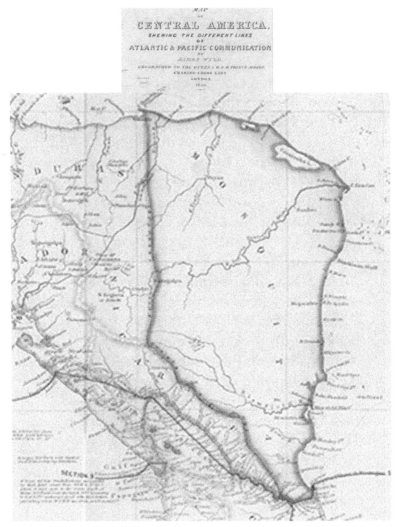

The Miskito presence was even greater. At the end of the 17th century, the Miskito presence was over the entire Atlantic Coast; from Cabo Honduras to the Chiriquí lagoon in Panama. The Miskitos made frequent raids along the Caribbean Coast, including Spanish settlements in Nicaragua, Costa Rica and Honduras. With these incursions they made indirect claim of dominion over these territories.

45

Control of our territory began to decrease with the intervention of the United States in the affairs of Mesoamerica. The Clayton-Bulwer Treaty of 1850 between the United States and Great Britain was the beginning. Followed by the Cruz-Wyke Treaty (1859) between Great Britain and Honduras, which ceded the northern portion of the Miskito Kingdom to Honduras. Then came the Treaty of Managua in 1860 between Great Britain and Nicaragua, for which Great Britain granted Nicaragua sovereignty (without Miskito Approval); the Miskito people vehemently opposed the treaty.

But later in 1894, the Nicaraguan government under José Santos Zelaya, invaded the country and used deception and force to make the alleged Miskito representatives to sign a Convention (See the appendix – *Mosquita Convention*) to cede sovereignty to Nicaragua. Despite that, resistance against the Nicaraguan occupation remained. But the end of everything was when the Altamirano-Harrison Treaty was signed between Nicaragua and Great Britain on April 19, 1905. In this treaty, the British finally accepted Nicaragua's sovereignty over the Moskitia. Although the British granted such a concession, it has not been the case with the Miskitos. The **Miskito people and patriots have never ceded their territory to Nicaragua**.

We must be clear that at no time before these treaties the Miskito territory of Honduras and Nicaragua were part of these countries. These governments have misrepresented our history and accommodated it according to their interests. Both use the term "re-incorporation of the Mosquitia" (sic), when the historical truth is that it had never been part of these countries. Nicaragua and Honduras are illegally and immorally occupying our ancestral land.

I believe that today more than ever, the new generation of Miskitos, with the advent of cyber communication, the multiplication of Miskito professionals in almost all branches of knowledge, the personal experience of many Miskitos in countries like the United States, and the acquisition of wealth by some, is forging a renewed feeling and drive for the establishment of the Miskito homeland. **The aspiration of the Miskito nation cannot be thwarted by treaties, atrocities, injustice, colonialism, and genocide.**

> I believe that today more than ever, the new generations of Miskitos, with the advent of cyber communication, the multiplication of Miskito professionals in almost all branches of knowledge, the personal experience of many Miskitos in countries like the United States, and the acquisition of wealth by some, it is forging a renewed feeling and drive for the establishment of the Miskito homeland.

It is important to mention again that the Moskitia is equivalent to 60 percent of the territory of what is now Nicaragua. That is why Nicaraguans do everything to keep us under their yoke. Without the occupation of the Moskitia by Nicaragua and Honduras; our territory would probably be the largest country in Central America. Many Miskitos believe that we are descendants of Abraham, the father of the Jewish and Christian faith; and as such, we connect our struggle with that of the Jews. Just as they were able to establish their homeland after 2500 years of occupation by different world powers, the same will happen to us. There is no injustice that will last forever. It's just a matter of time before God will intervene and punish the evil doers.

It is important to mention again that the Moskitia is equivalent to 60 percent of the territory of what is now Nicaragua. That is why Nicaraguans do everything to keep us under their yoke.

Without the occupation of the Moskitia by Nicaragua and Honduras; our territory would probably be the largest country in Central America

There is no injustice that will last forever. It's just a matter of time before God will intervene and punish the evil doers.

Historical Miskito Territory

This map shows the historical territory of the Miskito Kingdom. There are many historical documents attesting to this fact. Nicaragua was not even a country when this territory was recognized as belonging to the Miskito Kingdom.

MISKITO TERRITORY - HISTORICALLY

The Miskito territory was divided into 4 districts: the district of the general, the king, the governor and the admiral. The function of each of them was to protect the population from foreign forces, protect Miskito sovereignty, and maintain order in the communities.

**Miskito Territory
Political Division
XIII-XIX Century**

Source:

The Sambo and Tawira Miskitu: The Colonial Origins and Geography of Intra-Miskitu Differentiation in Eastern Nicaragua and Honduras.

https://www.researchgate.net/figure/Figure-Four-districts-of-the-Miskitu-Kingdom-circa-Authors-drawing_fig3_31267583

This map shows the presence and claim of authority made by the Miskito King. This was recognized by England by many decades before the forced annexation to Honduras and Nicaragua.

LA MOSQUITIA
según Inglaterra

Source:
https://panahistoria.files.wordpress.com/2010/10/reino-de-la-mosquitia.jpg.web.7/26/19.

This map was made after the forced annexation of the Moskitia. Even so, it clearly shows the territorial limits of the Miskitos.

Map of Moravian missions 1899

This map shows the territory claimed by MISURASATA – it was obviously less than the historical limits.

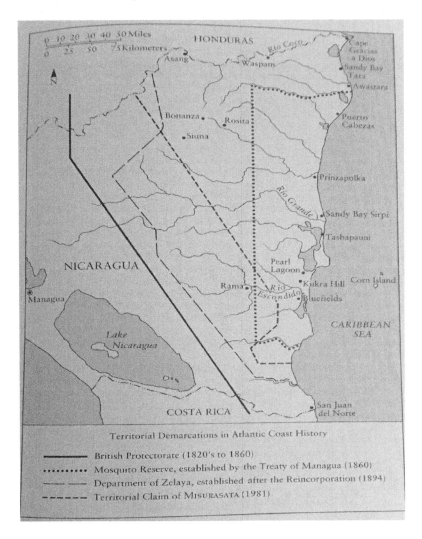

Territorial Demarcations in Atlantic Coast History

———— British Protectorate (1820's to 1860)
•••••••••• Mosquito Reserve, established by the Treaty of Managua (1860)
— — — Department of Zelaya, established after the Reincorporation (1894)
- - - - - Territorial Claim of MISURASATA (1981)

This is the current map of the Moskitia of Nicaragua. Notice how the Nicaraguan government removed part of the territory of the Moskitia by awarding it to the departments of Rio San Juan, Matagalpa, and Jinotega. This is one example of how the supposed Regional Autonomy law[17] is negative for the indigenous groups of the Moskitia.

NICARAGUA XXI Century

Notice how the Nicaraguan government reduced part of the territory of the Moskitia by awarding it to the departments of Rio San Juan, Matagalpa, and Jinotega.

[17] LEY N°. 28 *"ESTATUTO DE AUTONOMÍA DE LAS REGIONES DE LA COSTA ATLÁNTICA DE NICARAGUA"* (1987, 2003, 2016)

Key Dates in Our History

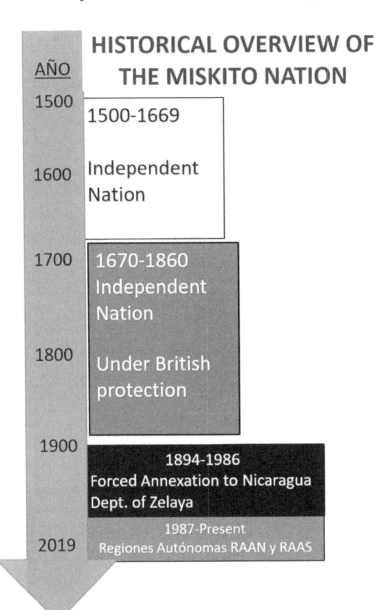

AÑO

HISTORICAL OVERVIEW OF
THE MISKITO NATION

AÑO	
1500	**1500-1669**
1600	Independent Nation
1700	**1670-1860** Independent Nation
1800	Under British protection
1900	**1894-1986** Forced Annexation to Nicaragua Dept. of Zelaya
2019	**1987-Present** Regiones Autónomas RAAN y RAAS

MISKITO NISANKA STURKALUPIA

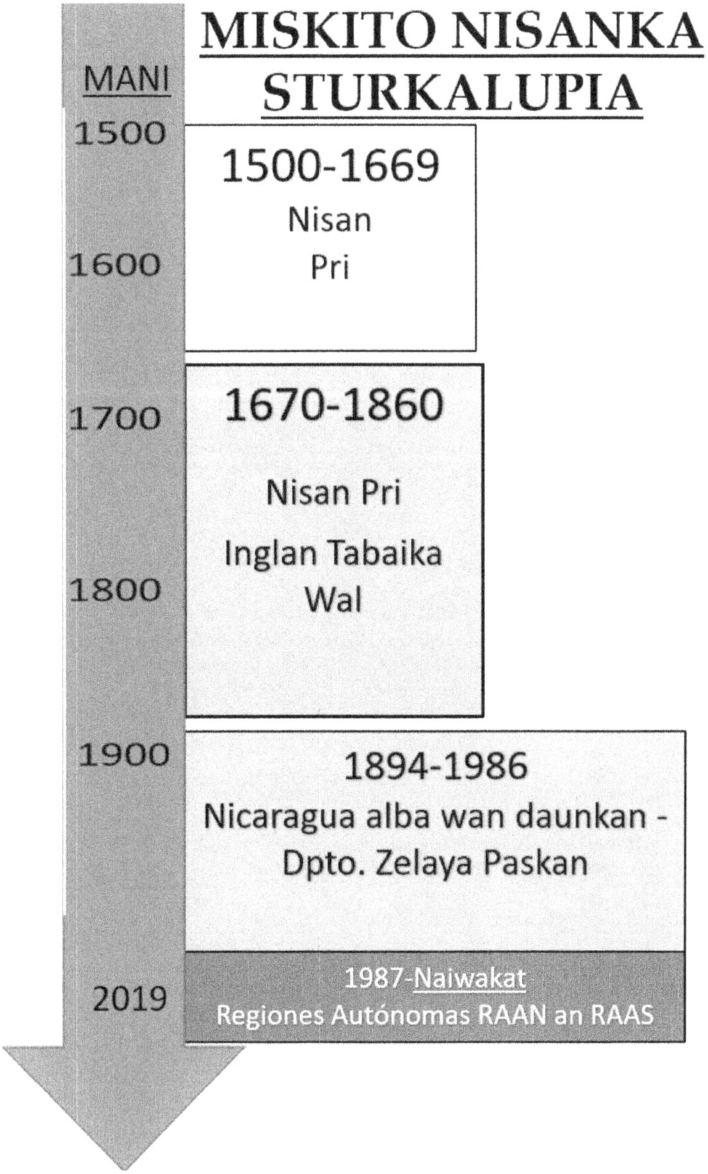

MANI

1500

1500-1669

Nisan

1600

Pri

1700

1670-1860

Nisan Pri

Inglan Tabaika

1800

Wal

1900

1894-1986

Nicaragua alba wan daunkan -

Dpto. Zelaya Paskan

2019

1987-Naiwakat

Regiones Autónomas RAAN an RAAS

Fig 1

KEY DATES IN THE HISTORY OF THE MISKITU PEOPLE

YEARS 1500'S

- In 9/12/1502- Christopher Columbus takes refuge in the Miskito territory - Calls the place, *Cabo Gracias a Dios.*
- In 1512- The King of Spain Fernando sends an expedition with a Governor to seize the Miskito territory but the natives expel them.
- In 1522 and 1523 - Spain launches attacks from its colonial territories - Guatemala and Honduras, but they also fail. The Spaniards call the Miskitos, "Brave Indians."

Source: Muller, A. Karl. *Among Creoles, Miskitos and Sumos.* The Comenius Press. Bethlehem, PA. 1932.
Olien, Michael D.. *The Miskito Kings and the Line of Succession.* Department of Anthropology, University of Georgia, Athens, GA. *Journal of Anthropological Research* 39.2 (1983): 198–241

Fig 2

YEARS 1600'S

- At the beginning of the 1600's Spain tries again to seize the Miskito territory using another strategy; the use of Roman Catholic missionaries, but once again, they failed.
- In 1625, **Dama** (Old Man) is recognized as the King of the Miskito Nation.

- In 1670 the Miskitos asked to be under the protectorate of England; King James of England; recognizes the Miskito "Chief" as the ruler of the Moskitia.

- In 1688 the naturalist Sir Hans Sloane witnesses the visit of the Miskito King Jeremy I to Jamaica.

Source: Muller, A. Karl. *Among Creoles, Miskitos and Sumos.* The Comenius Press. Bethlehem, PA. 1932.
Olien, Michael D.. *The Miskito Kings and the Line of Succession.* Department of Anthropology, University of Georgia, Athens, GA. *Journal of Anthropological Research* 39.2 (1983): 198–241

Fig 4

YEARS 1800'S

- In 1800 Miskito General Robinson attacks the Black River fortress forcing the withdrawal of the brief Spanish presence on Miskito land.

- In 1847 Moravian missionaries begin their work in the Moskitia.

- In 1860 The Treaty of Managua is signed.

- In 1894 Bluefield is invaded; the Miskito Kingdom is forcefully annexed to Nicaragua.

Source:
- Conzemius Eduard. *Ethnographical survey of the Miskito and Sumu Indians of Honduras and Nicaragua*. 1932. Smithsonian Institution Bureau of American Ethnology. Bulletin 106. Washington, D.C
- Muller, A. Karl. *Among Creoles, Miskitos and Sumos*. The Comenius Press. Bethlehem, PA. 1932.
- Olien, Michael D.. *The Miskito Kings and the Line of Succession*. Department of Anthropology. University of Georgia, Athens, GA. *Journal of Anthropological Research* 39.2 (1983): 198–241

Fig 3

YEARS 1700'S

- In 1720 the Miskitos seek help from Great Britain and enter into a formal treaty; the establishment of English colonies in Miskito territory is allowed.
- In 1725 for the second time, naturalist Sir Hans Sloane witnesses the visit of the Miskito King to Jamaica.

- In 1745 The Anglican Church makes its presence in the Moskitia.

- In 1783 as part of the Treaty of Versailles, Britain ordered all its subjects to leave Moskitia.

- In 1796 the Spaniards settled in the fortress of Rio Negro.

Source:
- Conzemius Eduard. *Ethnographical survey of the Miskito and Sumu Indians of Honduras and Nicaragua*. 1932. Smithsonian Institution Bureau of American Ethnology. Bulletin 106. Washington, D.C
- Muller, A. Karl. *Among Creoles, Miskitos and Sumos*. The Comenius Press. Bethlehem, PA. 1932.
- Reneouf, W. Robert. *Anglicanismo en Nicaragua 1745-1985*. *Anglican and Episcopal History*. Vol. 57, No. 4 (December 1988).

1900-1907 - Under the leadership of Sam Pitts, the Miskitos try to get help from Britain and the US to restore their independence.
In 1905 the Harrison Altamirano Treaty (Nicaragua-England) was signed by which communal land titles were granted to indigenous peoples.

YEARS 1900'S

1928-1929 the Miskitos help the US Marines to pursue Augusto Cesar Sandino.

In 1974 Moravian pastors created ALPROMISU - Alliance for the Progress of the Miskitus and Sumus
In November 1979 MISURASATA is created – *Miskitu, Sumu, Rama, Sandinista Aslatakanka*
In February of 1981, the Sandinistas try to arrest a Miskito leader in Prinzapolka, members of the Miskito literacy campaign participants rallies; four Miskitos and four Sandinista soldiers die in the incident.
In January 1982, the Sandinistas forcibly relocated 10,000 Miskito from the banks of the Coco River, in concentration camps located further south, and destroyed no less than 100 Miskite communities.

Source: *Pueblos Indígenas y Tradicionales y Áreas Protegidas - Reserva Biológica Marina de Cayos Miskitos y Franja Costera, Nicaragua*. Publicado por UICN, Gland, Suiza y Cambridge, Reino Unido y WWF International, Gland, Suiza. Edson A. Merritt (Capt USMC). *U.S. Marines and Miskito Indians, the Rio Coco patrol of 1928*. USMC, Nicaragua, August 1928. https://mca-marines.org/leatherneck/nicaragua-1928-the-rio-coco-patrol/

YEARS 2000'S

On April 19, 2009, the Council of Elders of the Miskito nation announces its unilateral independence from Nicaragua; **Miskito Community Nation**, is the name given to the new Miskito state.
2019, settlers continue to invade Miskito and Mayagna lands – THE FIGHT CONTINUES

A Territory Under Occupation

The Miskito Kingdom became part of Nicaragua's sovereignty on November 20, 1894. After the Nicaraguan government militarily occupied Bluefields and forced King Clarence into exile, the Nicaraguan government named the Miskito territory, the department of Zelaya. Afterwards established their invading general Rigoberto Cabezas as governor. The Miskitos and the Creoles vehemently opposed all the actions of José Santos Zelaya.

59

To give legitimacy to his occupation and usurpation, Zelaya organized a convention led by Cabezas. For this they prepared in advance a "decree of re-incorporation", to be signed by the "representatives" of the Moskitia. In said decree or convention[18] (**See Appendix 1 to read the convention and a personal commentary**), you can read the nefarious, dishonest and immoral language used by the Nicaraguans. Moreover, in their perversion and immorality, Cabezas and Zelaya made use of the oath to God and the Bible to carry out their injustice; they knew very well that it was a farce. Yet, as immoral individuals, they were not afraid to use God's name and the Word for their evil purposes.

To use God and His holy Name to commit injustice invokes His wrath and punishment. This may be one of the reasons why Nicaragua suffers from frequent calamities and has lived under dictators such as Zelaya, the Somoza's and Ortega.

> To use God and His holy Name to commit injustice invokes His punishment. This may be one of the reasons why Nicaragua suffers from frequent calamities and has lived under dictators such as Zelaya, the Somoza's and Ortega.

Cabezas used the Miskitos who were brought to Bluefields by force by the soldiers, to complete his evil intentions. He deceived them, gave them alcoholic beverages for several days and in that state, he made them put their fingers in a decree written in Spanish, in a language they did not and could not understand. This event is well known among our Miskito people. That is

---

[18] The Convention was obviously a document aimed to make the Nicaraguan government look good. This convention was immoral and illegal, as there was no genuine representation.

why the idea of seeking independence persists; **we believe that we are a territory under occupation.**

It is important to emphasize that after the so called "convention", most Miskitos were disgusted and angry about what had happened. Although some chose to submit to the occupation. It is very likely that this was due to the presence of Nicaraguan soldiers in Bluefields and other parts of the Moskitia. At that time, the Miskito army no longer existed. Since the King had been violently removed, there was confusion and lack of leadership in the nation; add to that the lack of channels of communication which made it very difficult to report what had happened.

Even so, some heard the news and chose to rebel civically, diplomatically and even militarily. The most prominent leader in all this was the hero **Sam Pitts**. He did everything possible to maintain the hope of re-establishing Miskito independence. The following letter from Pitts contains the feeling of the Miskito population at that time. In his letter to the British government in January 1901 he wrote:

> *The inhabitants were satisfied with their local government and had no desire to be Nicaraguans ... Therefore we strongly protested the occupation of our Nation (Reservation) and the subsequent transformation of it; this has been a flagrant violation of the Treaty of Managua of 1860 which was agreed by the Government of Her Majesty the Queen.*

There are enough historical documents to indicate that the Miskito people never agreed with the supposed and badly called reinstatement of the Moskitia. There must be a remedy for this injustice, one way or another.

3
THE CONSTANT STRUGGLE
M K (Miskut Kiamka)

A review of history shows us that the Miskito people have lived in a constant struggle to keep their ethnic, communal, cultural, linguistic, and territorial identity. We are finishing the second decade of the 21st century and the fight continues. While other indigenous groups have assimilated into the dominant culture, the Miskito nation continues to resists. For there is a strong feeling and concept among our people in the sense that God gave us our ethnic identity and territory; therefore, we have a responsibility to take care of it.

Spirit of Survival

As Conzemius indicates, the Miskitos have been warriors by nature. In the past, all men were considered soldiers in the event of conflict (81). From that spirit of struggle and determination, the concept of *Taplu* or *Tahplu* is born; Tahplu is the name given to war heroes. In the Miskito idiomatic we say: "Witin ba Taplu sika; he is a hero or brave". This concept led many young people

> From that spirit of struggle and determination, the concept of Taplu or Tahplu is born; Tahplu is the name given to war heroes. In the Miskito idiomatic we say: "*Witin ba Taplu sika*; he is a hero or brave man".

to join the military struggle against the Sandinista government in the 1980s.

Historical anecdotes indicate that the Miskitos were (and are) skilled, bold and brave in war. There are numerous writings that indicate that the Miskitos were the indigenous nation with the greatest presence and military power in the Caribbean coast region from Honduras to Panama. There is no information on the number of members of the Miskito army, but everything indicates that there was a military force defending the Kingdom. This army ceased to exist when the 1860 treaty was signed (Olien 235). The evidence show that the Miskito nation operated as a regional power that forcefully confronted the Spanish conquistadors. Miskitos and many natives were so anti Spain probably because of the well-known barbarism that the Spaniards committed when they arrived in indigenous lands.

Although they were skilled at using traditional indigenous weapons, the Miskito leaders realized they needed firearms to defend themselves. Over the years, the Miskito kings, to protect their territory and people, established alliances with the British, the French and Dutch buccaneers, to obtain firearms. This made their forces more formidable than that of other indigenous peoples. Helms is of the opinion that other indigenous nations in the area were very afraid of the Miskitos (194). It is likely that this was due primarily to the fact that the Miskitos had firearms and also because once captured they were used as slaves.[19]

It is quite possible that the first military confrontation between Miskitos and Spaniards happened soon after Columbus arrived in Cabo Gracias

---

[19] **Slavery -** This practice was declared illegal by Miskito King Robert Charles Frederick in 1832.

a Dios. He notified the Spanish king about the Miskito land and its mining wealth. It happened that after his visit, Spain sent several contingents to take possession of the Moskitia. But the Miskito people defended itself from the invaders. As Rogers imply, in the 16th century, not many Spanish conquerors ventured into the area. Nevertheless, one that did so was Diego de Nicuessa in 1512, but his expedition was shipwrecked at the mouth of the Wanki River (Coco River), near Cabo Gracias a Dios (117). Attacks on the Miskito territory followed in the years 1522 and 1523, which were launched from Honduras and Guatemala, but were also rejected and defeated by the Miskitos.

Mueller affirms that the Spaniards changed tactics to take possession of the Miskito Coast. Instead of armed soldiers they used religious soldiers; they used Catholic monks. These were not really interested in proclaiming the Word of God or the expansion of His Kingdom; rather the expansion and establishment of the reign of the Catholic kings of Spain and the stealing of indigenous wealth. Due to the military and religious insistence of the Spaniards, the different Indian tribes (e.g. Miskitos, Sumos) put aside their differences to face the invading forces. Due to this united fierce resistance, the Spaniards gave up their efforts and called the inhabitants "brave Indians", thus indicating the respect they came to have for the spirit of survival of the Miskitos and Mayagnas (58).

The Caribbean coast between Honduras and Panama was the scene of many Miskito raids. Conzemius quotes Cockburn to indicate that the Miskitos invaded Chiriquí (Panama) in 1732. He also adds that in 1758, the Miskito forces captured other indigenous people near Bocas del Toro (83). Roberts writes that, in 1816, the "Brave Indians" of Panama paid tax or certain kind of tribute to the Miskito King (71). This infers that the Miskitos had presence and dominion over some of these tribes.

The Miskito forces were used by the English to confront their enemies in the Caribbean. Conzemius declares that on June 25, 1720, by agreement between the governor of Jamaica Sir Nicholas Lawes and the Miskito king Jeremy, the latter sent a contingent of 200 Miskitos to Jamaica. The purpose was to help the governor track down the Maroons (Descendants of Blacks and mulattos) who had fled to the mountains seeking their freedom. Then in 1725, the English captain Robert Lade took "100 Muscheto Indians" [sic] to Jamaica to fight the Maroons. The Miskitos sent another contingent of 200 soldiers in 1738 to achieve the surrender of the Maroons (Conzemius 86-87). I mention these events only to underline the recognition that the Miskitos were considered capable, skilled, brave and effective fighters and great in tracking and confronting their enemies.

There is a historical account that I love because it describes the historically indomitable spirit of the vast majority of Miskitos. History shows that our struggle to survive is unquestionable. Up to a point, we are like the Jewish people; we fight with faith and determination. One of these days God will give us a Moses, a Joshua or a Moshe Dayan, so we can obtain our independence. It's just a matter of time.

In the following story, Dampier tells about a Miskito they had left on Juan Fernández Island, in the South Pacific Ocean.

> March the 22nd, 1684, we came in sight of
> the Island, and the next day got in and
> anchored in a Bay at the South end of the

Island, in 25 fathom[20] water, not two Cables lengths from the shore. We presently got out our canoa, and went ashore to see for a *Moskito (sic)* Indian, whom we left here when we were chaced (sic) hence by three Spanish ships in the year 1681, a little before we went to *Arica;* Captain Watlin being then our commander, after Captain *Sharp* was turned out.

This Indian lived here alone above 3 years, and altho he was several times sought after by the Spaniards, who knew he was left on the Island, yet they could never find him. He was in the Woods hunting for goats, when Captain Watlin drew off his men, and the ship was under sail before he came back to shore. He had with him his gun and a knife, with a small horn of powder, and a few shot; which being spent, he contrived a way by notching his knife, to saw the barrel of his gun into small pieces, wherewith he made harpoons, lances, hooks, and a long knife; heating the pieces first in the fire, which he struck with his gunflint, and a piece of the barrel of his gun, which he hardened; having learnt to do that among the English. The hot pieces of iron he would hammer out and bend as he pleased with stones, and saw them with his jagged knife, or grind them to an edge by long

---

[20] **Fathom** – A unit of length equal to six feet (1.83 meters) used especially for measuring the depth of water.

labour, and harden them to a good temper, as there was occasion.

All this may seem strange to those that are not acquainted with the sagacity of the Indians; but it is no more than these Moskito men are accustomed to in their own Country, where they make their own fishing and striking Instruments, without either Forge or Anvil; tho they spend a great deal of time about them.

Other wild Indians who have not the use of Iron, which the Moskito men have from the English, make hatchets of a very hard stone, with which they will cut down trees, (the Cotton Tree especially, which is a soft tender Wood) to build their Houses or make Canoas; and though in working their Canoas hollow, they cannot dig them so neat and thin, yet they will make them fit for their service. This their digging or hatchet-work they help out by fire; whether for the felling of the trees, or for the making the inside of their canoa hollow...

But to return to our Moskito man on the Isle of John Fernando. With such instruments as he made in that manner, he got such provision as the island afforded; either goats or fish. He told us that at first, he was forced to eat seal, which is very ordinary meat, before he had made hooks: but afterwards he never kill'd any seals but to make lines, cutting their skins into thongs. He had a little house or hut half a mile from the sea, which was lined with goats skin; his couch or barbecu of sticks lying along about 2 foot distant from the ground, was spread with the same, and was all his Bedding. He had no cloaths left, having worn out those he brought from Watlin's Ship, but only a skin about his waste. He saw our ship the day before we came to an Anchor, and did believe we were English, and therefore kill'd 3 Goats in the morning, before we came to an anchor, and drest them with cabbage, to treat us when we came ashore.

He came then to the sea side to congratulate our safe arrival. And when we landed, a Moskito Indian named *Robin*, first leapt ashore, and running to his brother Moskito man, threw himself flat on his face at his feet; who helping him up and embracing him, fell flat with his face on the ground at *Robins* feet, and was by him taken up also. We stood with pleasure to behold the surprize and tenderness, and solemnity of this interview, which was exceedingly affectionate on both sides; and when their ceremonies of civility were over, we also that stood gazing at them drew near, each of us embracing him we had found here, who was overjoyed to see so many of his old friends come hither, as he thought, purposely to fetch him. He was named *Will,* as the other was *Robin.* (Dampier 85-87)

This story tells about attitudes that are much appreciated and common among our people. We have a survival instinct. We know how to survive in the forest or near the sea. We are also loyal to our friends. And as

Meeting with a Miskito Indian, Caspar Luyken, Abraham de Hondt, 1698 - Image ID: RYEC4J

Encuentro con un Indio Miskito, Caspar Luyken, Abraham de Hondt, 1698

the story describes, we enjoy each other when we see one of us who we had not seen for years. This custom tends to be more common among the young and elderly women. They hug you; they kiss you; they talk to you with love, and they even cry while talking about the times she thought of you. I have experienced this many times. The other Miskito brothers who live abroad and have returned to visit can testify of this.

In 1928, Edson A. Merritt, a captain of the United States Marines, describes the spirit and attitude of the Miskitos, which has not changed. Merritt wrote:

> The Miskitos prided themselves on not having been subjugated by the first Spanish adventurers. Nor had they assimilated into Nicaraguan culture, but were more than determined to remain in the domain of the dense jungle, a nation within a nation that saw Nicaraguans as "Spaniards." They were the absolute owners of a vast region of rainforest, the second of its kind. Immensity that can only be attributed to the Amazon, almost without roads and with few paths. In this extremely remote area known as "The Frontier," the Miskitos, unsurpassed sailor experts, roamed freely along waterways that would have defeated anyone else.

"The Miskitos prided themselves on not having been subjugated by the first Spanish adventurers. Nor had they assimilated into Nicaraguan culture, but were more than determined to remain in the domain of the dense jungle, a nation within a nation that saw Nicaraguans as "Spaniards."". Merritt

---

In his instructions to his Marines, Edson, referring to the Miskitos, said: "The Miskitos are proud people with a long history. Our success depends on your assistance. They are much better sailing this river than any of us. Only by dealing with them man to man, can we honestly have any hope of success. I hope each of you will conduct yourself that way. I think that if we offer them our true friendship, they will accept it." (Merritt 1928)

The following year, another Marine instructor in Bluefields made an assessment of the Miskito warrior, he commented the following: "I cannot conceive of a soldier more valuable than a Mosquito [sic] child trained and disciplined on the property (*usage of weapons*) with his knowledge of woodwork and tracking and, at the same time, the ability to read a simple map and perhaps make a simple sketch."(Brooks 1929 – Italics added) These comments reveal the indomitable spirit of our people; a spirit that fell asleep over the years under occupation, indoctrination, forced assimilation, and discrimination by the Nicaragua people and government.

"I cannot conceive of a soldier more valuable than a Mosquito [sic] child trained and disciplined on the property (*usage of weapons*) with his knowledge of woodwork and tracking and, at the same time, the ability to read a simple map and perhaps make a simple sketch" Instructor of the US Marines.

The Eighties War

The indomitable spirit of the Miskito people was markedly displayed in the 1980's war. The sleeping spirit of the Miskitos was awakened when the Nicaraguan government, this time in the hands of the Sandinistas, wanted to impose the dominant culture and implant the Marxist-Leninist ideology on the Miskito Coast. Faith in God, the historical claim of autonomy, cultural difference with the rest of Nicaragua, and the Miskito identity clashed with the imposing effort of the Sandino-communist government.

Before the arrival of the Sandinistas, the Nicaraguan government, through its dictator in turn, Anastasio Somoza, had a "friendly" relationship with the Miskitos. The motto of his government towards the Coast was, "Kupia Kumi", one heart or feeling. He promised many things, but he did very little. However, a cultural, ideological and military imposition was not experienced in the Moskitia like the one intended by the new Sandinista dictatorship. When many applauded the Sandinistas inside and outside the country, the Miskitos had already detected who they really were; stealers, totalitarians, intolerants, and human rights violators.

After the Nicaraguan government came under the control of the Sandinistas on July 19, 1979, the new government actively began to incorporate Nicaragua's Atlantic Coast (The Moskitia) into the so-called Sandinista revolution. The relative autonomy that the Miskitos lived under the Somoza regime was shaken. The Sandinistas, seemingly unaware or ignorant of the idiosyncrasy, feeling and history of the Moskitia, decided and insisted on incorporating it to impose Marxist values. This created resentment and rebellion of many of its inhabitants. This animosity was further exacerbated when the government began to bring into the Moskitia, communist Cubans and other internationalists for the purpose of indoctrinating our people.

72

> The Sandinistas, out of vengeance, arrogance or ignorance of the Miskito idiosyncrasy and patriotism and that of the inhabitants of the Moskitia, decided and insisted on incorporating it to impose their Marxist values.

It is possible that the Sandinistas could have achieved their intentions had it not been for the strong resistance and leadership of the Miskito leaders, MISURASATA members and the Costeño (Moskitia) people in general. It turns out that the literacy campaign in Miskito had awakened a new vision for Moskitia.

> It is possible that the Sandinistas could have achieved their intentions had it not been for the strong resistance and leadership of the Miskito leaders, MISURASATA members and the Costeño (Moskitia) people in general.

As part of that effort, I remember the great joy it felt to know that we were finally going to claim our autonomy with great determination. The completion of the multilanguage literacy campaign on February 20, 1981 would also bring the proclamation and claim of autonomy of the Moskitia. But a day earlier, the Marxist government arrested the main leaders of MISURASATA (Stedman Fagoth, Brooklyn Rivera and others), accusing them of separatists, somocistas, counter-revolutionaries and CIA agents. With that action, the government initiated a great campaign of terror and death, directed especially against the Miskitos.

The joy and aspiration of the people was changed into pain, persecution, and death. The Sandinista government sent a military contingent to arrest a Miskito member of the literacy brigade, in the Miskito town of Prinzapolka. The brigade members were celebrating the end of the campaign in a church when the troops arrived. The soldiers entered the church with rage and with their machine guns loaded. The church and brigade members resisted the soldiers and their companions, the internationalists.

The incident transcended in confrontation and shooting between both sides; for the Miskitos had managed to take away some of the soldiers' weapons. The result was four dead Miskitos and four dead Sandinista soldiers. The brigadistas fled to the mountain being supported by the Miskito population. This is how the armed rebellion against the Nicaraguan government began. Thousands of young people, children, women, and the elderly joined the war, directly and indirectly.

I still remember that night when news of what happened in Prinzapolka arrived. At that time, I lived in my hometown, Bilwi, and specifically in the El Cocal neighborhood. I was only a teenager but was a Miskito language literacy teacher in my neighborhood. That night, a large contingent of Sandinista army cronies arrived at barrio el Cocal, to arrest Roberto Wilson, who was one of the leaders of MISURASATA. Many children, young and elderly people from the neighborhood came to surround the heavily armed soldiers. There were dozens of us from the barrio. These were hours of anxiety that lasted for many years. I still remember when an elderly woman, whom I do not recall by name, went and held the arm and machine gun of the soldier directing the operation. She shook him and told him with a firm voice that she was willing to give her life for the freedom of her people. That action caused the soldiers to change their belligerent attitude.

There were many other similar cases in Bilwi and all over the Moskitia. Bilwi was long besieged by elements of the army and members of the sinister Policía de Orden Internon(POI). However, young people from different Christian denominations met in churches to pray for the situation, to show moral support for those who were fighting for the dignity and freedom of the Miskito people, and also to show that we were not afraid of them. We constantly marched in protest despite the fact that many were made to disappear(killed) or imprisoned. I still remember one of the slogans: "Only the Indian saves the Indian"; "Indian baman indian ra swaki sakisa".

I still remember one of the slogans:
"Only the Indian saves the Indian"
"Indian baman indian ra swaki sakisa".

The following year, in December 1982, the Sandinista army forcibly removed some 10,000 Miskitos (including women and children) who lived in the scattered villages along the Coco River, on the border with Honduras. They were taken to concentration camps

The following year, in December 1982, the Sandinista army forcibly removed some 10,000 Miskitos (including women and children) who lived in the scattered villages along the Coco River, on the border with Honduras. They were taken to concentration camps toward the center of the Coast. There they lived there many months in sludge; homeless, hungry and deprived of freedom; some were raped, tortured and killed.

towards the center of the Coast. There they lived there many months in sludge; homeless, hungry and deprived of freedom; some were raped, tortured and killed.

But none of that frightened them. The majority continued with their fighting spirit. By expelling them from their villages, the Nicaraguan army burned their homes and entire communities and killed dozens of Miskitos. There is enough evidence to point out that the Nicaraguan government committed crimes against humanity against the Miskito people. These actions caused more Miskitos to join the rebel forces and others sought refuge in the Miskito communities of Honduras. Stedman Fagoth became the main leader of the Miskito rebels of Misura led by Wycliff Diego. Later another group was formed; Kisan. Both rebel groups operated from bases in the Honduran Moskitia. MISURASATA operated from Costa Rica under the command of Brooklyn Rivera.

> There is enough evidence to point out that the Nicaraguan government committed crimes against humanity against the Miskito people.

The brave struggle of the Miskitos attracted worldwide attention and led leaders of other indigenous ethnic groups in America to join. The indomitable spirit of the Miskito people and their determination to obtain their self-determination forced the Marxist government of Nicaragua to dialogue and legislate a law of autonomy that is useless.

The brave struggle of the Miskitos attracted worldwide attention and led leaders of other indigenous ethnic groups in America to join.

Hundreds of Miskitos were forcefully removed from their communities and were taken to concentrations camps. (called "asentamientos" by the Sandinistas)

UN EJEMPLO DE MUCHOS – ONE OF MANY EXAMPLES

Una casa Miskita es incendiada por el ejercito Sandinista durante el infame operativo militar conocido como "Navidad Roja". Decenas de Miskitos fueron asesinados en el operativo que tuvo lugar entre 1981-82.

A Miskito house is set on fire by the Sandinista army during the infamous military operation known as "Navidad Roja" (Red Christmas). Dozens of Miskitos were killed in that operation that took place between 1981-82.

2018 - Miskitos take up arms to defend themselves against the colonists (settlers) , who are former members of the Sandinista army and police and Liberal Party supporters of Arnoldo Alemán (former Nicaraguan President).

KNOWN CONCENTRATION CAMPS ("Asentamientos"; Tasba Pri) ESTABLSIHED BY THE SANDINISTAS TO SUPRESS THE MISKITOS

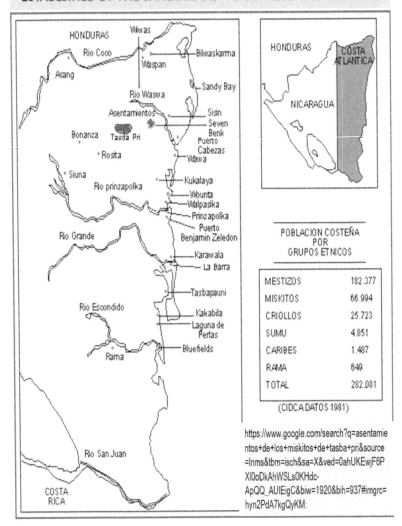

POBLACION COSTEÑA POR GRUPOS ETNICOS

MESTIZOS	182.377
MISKITOS	66.994
CRIOLLOS	25.723
SUMU	4.851
CARIBES	1.487
RAMA	649
TOTAL	282.081

(CIDCA DATOS 1981)

Certainly, the war against the Sandinista dictatorship in the 1980s speaks of many heroic acts of the Miskitos; Men and women of all ages. The genocide that the Nicaraguan government tried to carry out, made the fighting spirit of the Miskito nation to revive. Before that horrible situation, our people through its leaders only spoke, but did not act. That attitude has changed.

We are about to end the second decade of the 21st century and the situation of our people has not improved. We often hear news about murdered Miskitos by the heavily armed settlers that occupy their lands. This happens with the approval of the Nicaraguan government, which has shown no interest in improving the situation of our people.

The Miskito people has suffered tremendously under the Nicaraguan occupation. The worst administrations have been those led by the Liberal Party and the Sandinista Front. From the liberal José Santos Zelaya to the Sandinista Daniel Ortega, our people have endured many violent events. Yet the international community only talks about it but does not take action. So, we have to continue in our fight; *for only an Indian saves an Indian*. There have been murders, persecutions, tortures, and disappearances at the hands of the Nicaraguan government; but our struggle has not and will not cease.

Thus, the creation of a non-partisan Miskito Community Police force is very much needed; to ensure the security of our citizens and territorial integrity of the Miskito, Mayagna, and other communities. This is not something that the Nicaraguan government through its army and police wishes to accomplish. In fact, they are the problem. They are an occupation force.

The creation of a non-partisan **Miskito Community Police force** is very much needed; to ensure the security of our citizens and territorial integrity of the Miskito, Mayagna and other communities.

The Miskito people is a God-fearing (Jehovah) people. I believe and pray that someday, the Almighty in His mercy and justice will raise a Miskito leader of the caliber of Martin Luther King Jr. or Moses; to lead us into the Promised Land (our self-determination). For God does not approve of those who commit injustice, murder and destroy and seek to destroy others to oppress or exterminate them.

This evil perpetrated by Nicaragua and Honduras is ending. I may not see the time when the Miskito people achieve its real autonomy, but I have faith and hope that God will make it happen. The reason is this; we are also children of our father Abraham. That is why I urge my Miskito brothers to seek the Great I Am wholeheartedly, for He is our only hope.

> I may not see the time when the Miskito people achieve their real autonomy, but I have faith and hope that God will make it happen, because we are also children of our father Abraham. That is why I urge my Miskito brothers to seek God wholeheartedly, for He is our only hope.

4
SPILLED BLOOD
M K (Miskut Kiamka)

A lot of Miskito blood has been shed in the last forty years. It is important to talk about this matter, as some researchers of our history only make a slight allusion to it. In the 1980s, the Sandinista government killed thousands, destroyed many Miskito villages and communities, and thousands were taken to concentration camps. Many Miskito mothers still mourn their children who disappeared as part of the repression and attempted genocide (see in youtube: *Nicaragua was Our Home*).[21]

Miskito blood is still spilled by settlers and also by the Nicaraguan police and army. The situation in Honduras, is less severe. We hope in God that one day this horrible experience comes to an end and that there may be a good relationship between nations. Nicaraguans and Hondurans should raise awareness and demand from their rulers a different attitude towards the Moskitia. This we pray and expect from the Almighty; therefore, we must not lose faith nor hope.

I strongly agree with Fallon that for the time being, Nicaragua is only interested in the *Nicaraguanization* of the Moskitia. He says the following about it:

---

[21] See the following video on YouTube, it confirms part of the horrors and pain of the Miskitos during the Sandinista era.
https://www.youtube.com/watch?v=xxySvhSt_Rk

The objective of Nicaraguan colonization is to alter the demography of the autonomous regions. It is about establishing a Nicaraguan `` majority '' so that, if the region was allowed to vote on independence, they could be defeated ``democratically''. This is the strategy that Morocco is currently using in Western Sahara. It is the same strategy previously used by Saddam Hussein in his ``Arabization '' campaign of Iraqi Kurdistan.

THE NICARAGUANIZATION OF THE MOSKITIA

The objective of Nicaraguan colonization is to alter the demography of the autonomous regions. It is about establishing a Nicaraguan `` majority '' so that, if the region was allowed to vote on independence, they could be defeated ``democratically''. This is the strategy that Morocco is currently using in Western Sahara. It is the same strategy previously used by Saddam Hussein in his ``Arabization '' campaign of Iraqi Kurdistan.

Prominent Miskitos
and Miskito Groups

Throughout our history, we have seen many prominent Miskitos emerge in different areas of life. Here I will mention some of them. In some cases, a figure will be used to highlight the sacrifice, labor, influence, and / or patriotism of a group. Let's start by giving the Miskito warrior the first mention; and especially those who gave their lives in the eighties, for the love of their people. Their sacrifice has resulted in a worldwide recognition of our tragedy in the hands of the Nicaraguan government. Their fierce fight and spilled blood forced the Nicaraguan government to legislate a law of autonomy (Law No. 28 (1987) "Statute of Autonomy of the Regions of the Atlantic Coast of Nicaragua),[22] which in reality is not worth the paper it is written on.

---

[22] **Note on the Law of Autonomy for the Moskitia.**

• A serious analysis of the autonomy law demonstrates that it is an instrument of the Nicaraguan government to divide the territory of the Moskitia into parts; It also intends to divide the inhabitants of the Moskitia so that they accept the government of Nicaragua as a legitimate government in the Moskitia. It is well known that this law, with its various revisions, is not being complied with and is biased to favor the central government.

• The governments on duty know that most of the Miskitos reject the presence of Nicaragua. Therefore, the central government has allowed settlers to usurp Miskito lands in order to strengthen their presence in the territory through settlers or former soldiers of the Nicaraguan government. The central government's support for political parties based in Managua, and the purchase of politicians from the Coast with privileges; this is another strategy to divide and minimize the political power of the Miskitos.

84

Before listing the most outstanding Miskitos and groups, it is important to mention that the Miskito nation has had bad children. All the peoples, tribes and nations of the world have experienced the shame of seeing that some of their members are traitors to their people. The Miskitos have suffered this shame. Some Miskitos have allied themselves with the oppressors and exploiters of our people.

> Some Miskitos have allied themselves with the oppressors and exploiters of our people.

These traitors are useful idiots and bad children. I think of them as immoral people, with no integrity and very little self-esteem. They are ungrateful and perhaps ignore the true history of our people. They are willing to sell their soul to the devil for "a few dollars more". In their foolishness, some believe in the lying words of national or colonial political leaders and their political parties. History has repeatedly demonstrated that they do not have the well-being of the Miskito people in mind. It is my hope and prayer that at some point, they come to the realization that we cannot trust these people.

1. The Miskito Warrior

It is important to recognize that the Miskito nation is still fighting for its autonomy and independence. This continues because we have Miskito children who are warriors. A special recognition must be given to the hundreds who gave their lives fighting against the Sandinista government of Nicaragua, led by Daniel Ortega, in the 1980s.

Miskito Rebel - A contra guerilla of the Miskito people, Nicaragua, 1987. The group was fighting in opposition to the Sandinista government. (Photo by Scott Wallace/Getty Images)

In the war against the communist Sandinistas, thousands of Miskitos were willing to give their life for patriotisms; for their love of the Miskito homeland. Among them was Commander Bruno Gabriel Peralta.

Source:
https://www.gettyimages.com/detail/news-photo/contra-guerilla-of-the-miskito-people-nicaragua-1987-the-news-photo/476982837.web.7/26/19.

Miskito Patriot

2. King Robert Henry Clarence

Clarence was our last king. He fought to maintain the independence of the Moskitia. This deserves our recognition.

> **Based on historical evidence, we can say that the Moskitia is a territory under occupation by foreign forces (Nicaragua and Honduras).**

Robert Henry Clarence - King of the Miskito Kingdom; he reigned from 1890 - 1894 - when he was forced into exile by the Nicaraguan government.

Read chapter 24 of *The Awakning Coast*, it tells the courage and rejection of the Miskito Chief and the population of Moskitia to the invasion and occupation of the military forces of Nicaragua. Based on historical evidence, we can say that the Moskitia is a territory under occupation of foreign forces.

Biography of King Robert Henry Clarence

King Robert Henry Clarence reigned from 1890 – 1894; in the later year, he was deposed by the Nicaraguan government through an invasion. He was the hereditary Chief of the Miskito people. Born at Rama Cay, Bluefields Lagoon, 6th September 1872, son of H.E. King William Henry Clarence, hereditary King of the Miskitos, by a lady from Rama. Educated at the Moravian Mission School, Bluefields.

He was proclaimed as *Hereditary Chief of the Miskitos* by the General Council on January 29th, 1891 (with effect from November 11th, 1890). He was crowned at Pearl City, on March 24th, 1891. Reigned under the guardianship of the Hon Charles Patterson, Vice-President of the Council, until he came of age and assumed full ruling powers on September 6th, 1893. He was forcefully deposed on February 12th, 1894, by the Nicaraguan army, after Bluefields was invaded. He was subsequently restored in July 6th, 1894 after British intervention. He was deposed again in the 7th of August 1894 after a second invasion, when all American and British residents were forcibly removed to Managua.

Later he was rescued by a British warship which took him into exile together with 200 refugees to Puerto Limon, Costa Rica, and later to Jamaica. By this time the British had agreed with the Nicaragua government to give them sovereignty over the Miskito Kingdom. He was repeatedly petitioned by his countrymen to return to the Miskito Coast to resume his reign, since most of the inhabitants of the Kingdom regarded him as their rightful King; this was the case throughout his exile. During this time, at least three rebellions were mounted against the Nicaraguan government. He died in Jamaica on the 6th of January 1908, due to illness.

From: Popular Science Monthly Volume 45, page 165 - (1894). FiG. 3. The Mosquito Chief and Executive Council: (1) Robert Henry Clarence, chief; (2) Hon. Charles Patterson, vice president and guardian; (3) Hon. J. W. Cuthbert, attorney general and secretary to the chief ; (4) Mr. J. W. Cuthbert, Jr. government secretary; (5) Mr. George Raymond, councilman and headman; (6) Mr. Edward McCrea, councilman and headman. Note that all but the two Black men are obvious Mulattoes

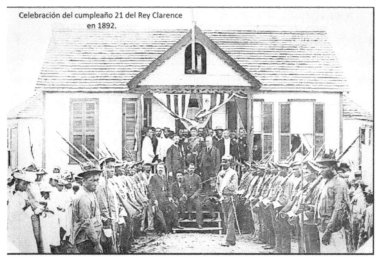

Celebration of the twenty-first birthday of Hereditary Chief Robert Henry Clarence at his house in Pearl Lagoon, 1892, showing Hon. J. Cuthbert to the chief 's left and several Moravians on the porch. From Feldballe, Views from the Mosquito Reservation, n.p. Courtesy of the California Digital Archive.

3. Sam Pitts

Sam Pitts is one of the many Miskito heroes; he was from the Yulu community, near Bilwi. In 1894, he rebelled against the Nicaraguan occupation. He made trips to Jamaica to persuade the king in exile to return to the Moskitia. He also sought the help of the British government regarding the Nicaraguan occupation. **But**

> **But the British cannot be trusted, they are not loyal to their friends, at least not to non-whites.**

the British cannot be trusted, they are not loyal to their friends, at least not to non-whites. Pitts was a leader who fought tirelessly to reestablish the independence of Moskitia. Because of his firm opposition, he was killed in 1907 by the Nicaraguan troops of Zelaya. The Nicaraguan government wanted to silence him since he also opposed in 1904 the illegal appointment of Andrew Hendy as honorary Chief to replace his cousin Henry Clarence.

4. Armstrong Wiggins

There are those who leave their homeland and forget their roots and their people, that is not the case with Wiggins. Despite living in the United States for many years, Wiggins has not forgotten his roots and his people. He has identified himself as Miskito and has defended his nation and the Miskito cause in various international forums. For this reason, we can say that he is one of the most prominent and illustrious Miskitos ever.

INDIAN LAW
RESOURCE CENTER

A Miskito with international influence; he has defended his people in different international forums. He is the director of the Washington, DC Office of the Indian Law Resource Center. He has testified on issues related to the rights of indigenous peoples in the Organization of American States and the United Nations.

Armstrong Wiggins

5. Brooklyn Rivera

Rivera was one of the main leaders of MISURASATA, which fought civic and then militarily to obtain the autonomy of the Miskitos, Sumos and Branches. In 1988, together with other indigenous leaders, he founded YATAMA, in order to continue fighting for Miskito autonomy. For his tireless struggle for the Miskitos, he is recognized as one of his most illustrious children.

Brooklyn Rivera

6. Dr. Kenneth Serapio Hunter

Dr. Serapio has helped his people and is a great example to follow. With much sacrifice he finished his medical study in Guatemala. He was jailed by the Sandinistas in 1984 and then went into exile. In Honduras he gave medical attention to Miskito refugees. This makes him deserving of recognition as one of the most prominent Miskitos.

7. ALPROMISU (Alliance for the progress of the Miskitos and Sumos)

The Alliance for the Progress of the Miskitos and Sumus deserves mention. This civic organization was created in May 1974 by the Miskito Moravian pastors in order to promote the welfare of the Miskitos and Sumos. That effort began the movement for the autonomy of the Moskitia. It disappeared in 1979 with the creation of MISURASATA.

8. MISURASATA (Miskito, Sumo, Rama, Sandinista Aslatakanka)

It can be said that this organization was the one that effectively promoted Nicaragua's recognition of the territorial rights of the natives of the Moskitia. Stedman Fagoth and Brooklyn Rivera were its main leaders. Due to the persecution of the Sandinista government of Nicaragua against the Miskito leaders and the arrest and murder of others, MISURASATA rebelled in arms against the government. This uprising has marked and demonstrated worldwide the indomitable spirit of the Miskito people. Everything that has resulted later with respect to the Moskitia is a product of this uprising.

In addition, the following Miskito pastors and leaders deserve mention:

- Gen. Lowry Robinson - General of the Miskito Forces; he defended Miskito sovereignty by serving under several Miskito kings.
- Silvio Diaz - Pastor
- Samuel Downs - Pastor
- Wycliff Diego - Pastor and rebel leader
- Bruno Gabriel Peralta - Rebel Commander

94

- Stedman Fagoth - He was one of the main leaders of MISURASATA

The Great Dream

Historically, for the vast majority of Miskitos, the great dream is to achieve self-determination, to become an independent state from Nicaragua. This dream lies in the fact that we (most Miskitos) have never considered ourselves Nicaraguans; and the state of Nicaragua itself with its exploitations and denigrations have reinforced this opinion.

Some Nicaraguans and some Miskitos, Creoles, Sumus and Ramas think that the idea of an independent homeland is a nonsense or something unattainable. But the reality is that no country is formed overnight, it always involves a long process of struggle (sometimes civic and military), sacrifice and death. Here are some examples of modern countries that emerged less than seventy-five years ago, **some only a decade ago**.

- **South Sudan** - On July 9, 2011, after a bloody civil war, South Sudan declared its independence from Sudan. The territory covers 644, 329 km²; it has 12,340,000 million inhabitants.
- **Kosovo** - On February 17, 2008, after a bloody war, Kosovo declared its independence from Serbia. The territory covers 10, 908 km² of surface; it has 1.8 million inhabitants.
- **East Timor** - On May 20, 2002, it became independent from Indonesia. The territory covers 15,410 km2; it has 1,167,000 million inhabitants.
- **Belize** - On September 21, 1981, Belize declared its independence from Great Britain (Guatemala claimed the territory for many decades). The

territory covers 22, 966 km²; it has 388,000 thousand inhabitants.

- **Israel** - On May 14, 1948, Israel declared its independence (rejecting British rule of its ancestral land). The territory covers 22,145 km²; it has 8, 900,000 million inhabitants.

The size of the Miskito territory (Nicaragua and Honduras) is approximately 65,000 km²; with a population of more than 700,000 people. With vast natural wealth, access to rivers and sea. With many virgin beaches that offer great potential for responsible tourism development. It is a country awaiting development and progress through an ethical community and Christian consciousness. A country where the common good must be above that of the individual or group.

The country of Moskitia would offer great opportunity for advancement and prosperity to its citizens. To be successful and to offer continual community advancement, it must operate in a proper balance between form[23] and freedom[24] (Schaeffer 309). The key is proper balance. We must avoid all extremes, as we see nowadays in Western democracies and totalitarian countries. These countries are plague with immorality, hatred, violence, corruption, rejection of truth, and the imposition of corrupted individual preferences over the masses. We must not allow the elite few to impose their will upon the people.

---

[23] **Freedom** – The capacity, faculty, will, and right of the people to choose without infringing on the right and wellbeing of others; to not be subject to the will or preferences of another individual.

[24] **Form** – Biblical morality and governmental laws, norms, guidelines, and discipline to which we owe and are ordered to adjust.

Moskitia inhabitants must continually keep in mind that freedom without proper balance of form will lead to chaos and form without proper balance of freedom will lead to totalitarianism. In summary, we should to seek to establish a country where all ethnic groups have voice. The Moskitia, governed by a moral community consciousness; a government that is organized, representative, and equitable, can offer all ethnic groups (Mayagnas, Ramas, Ladinos, Miskitos, Garifunas, and Creoles) the opportunity to work together to forge a better future for our community of nations and families.

Our Cosmovision

Despite being under the dominion of the Nicaraguan government for over a hundred years, from a general perspective, the Miskito people maintain a vision of self-identity and self-determination. For the Miskito people, the concept of a homeland is connected to the Miskito Kingdom and not with the state of Nicaragua. Miskito hope is deposited in the belief that, for being descendants of Abraham, the father of the Jewish Faith, one day, God will reward us with a better future.

The combination of faith and hope in God, our identity as a nation, and our spirit to fight for our rights and land, inspires the Miskito Nation to move forward fighting for a better future. The Miskito sees the world through the lens of faith in God, the God of Israel. Throughout the centuries, we have learned that our salvation and protection as a nation can only come from God. For the governments of Great Britain, the United States, Honduras, and Nicaragua have only wanted to use us for their own wicked purposes. By understanding this historical reality, we have the strong determination to encourage our children to have faith, to dream big, to study hard, work hard, and fight for a future homeland.

In the Process Towards Independence

The desire to be an independent nation from Nicaragua persists because of the marginalization, exploitation, discrimination, and usurpation we have suffered. If these attitudes and actions from the Nicaraguan government and people was to change, it is possible that this desire for independence would decrease and settle for a simple autonomy. But experience indicates that there is no political or moral will within the Nicaraguan society and government.

Most Miskitos agree that "Law No. 28 Statute of Autonomy of the Regions of the Atlantic Coast of Nicaragua" IS A FARCE. Rather, it was and it is another attempt to impose and strengthen Nicaraguan sovereignty over the Moskitia; by dividing its territory and population. This strategy has been used by the Russians and other governments over their occupied territories.

It is well known that the Nicaraguan government did not comply with the Treaty of Managua, the illegal Convention of 1894, nor has it complied with the Harrison - Altamirano Treaty. The Statute or Law of Autonomy of 1987 and its subsequent reforms (2003 & 2016) is useless. The natives of the Moskitia have not any benefits. This is another reason why the dream of independence from Nicaragua persists. A good example of this attitude was the *declaration of independence from Nicaragua; signed by the Miskito Council of Elders in 2009*. It is all part of a process towards true independence which may take another two decades.

I strongly believe that Miskito students, professionals, pastors and civic leaders have a moral obligation to seek the autonomy of the Moskitia. They must set aside their party affiliation and political ideology to advance the cause for self-determination. The injustice and the political, social and cultural immorality that the Nicaraguan government has promoted and tolerated must be confronted with determination; both nationally and internationally. Active resistance must continue. The strategy used by Dr. Martin Luther King Jr. in the United States is worthy of imitation.

The fighting continues and must continue. Although the Nicaraguan government has ignored it, the declaration of independence of the Council of Elders is internationally known. The Nicaraguan government has ignored this; they see it as a nonsensical rant by few old and ignorant Miskito elders. However, behind this declaration, there is more than a century old cry for freedom and independence. The desire of the Miskito Nation to be independent will persists. This action of the Council of Elders was another step towards the final goal.

News Reports

I will leave you with the following news reports about our struggle:

===

Letter to the Editor of The New York Times
17 February 1986

To the editor:

99

Almost all countries are armed against the citizens and the freedoms they claim. Nothing is revolutionary about the use of the armed forces to maintain an internal loyalty to the state.

His January 25 news article on the recent Sandinista air and land attacks against a joint investigation group of the Misurasata Indians and North American Indians traveling within the Miskito territory highlighted the recurring use of military power by Managua to force submission and destroy the resistance of the Indian peoples.

Russell Means, Hank Adams and Clem Chartier, American Indian leaders, are the first indigenous delegation to enter Miskito territory without Sandinista soldiers and translators. To locate and prevent the delegation from reporting its findings, Managua has once again resorted to armed violence against indigenous communities.

During several days of aerial bombardment and troop attacks against the Miskito peoples of Layasiksa, Lapan, Kukalaya and others southwest of Puerto Cabezas, the Sandinistas have broken the seven-month informal truce with the indigenous resistance forces, contradicting their own plan of autonomy for indigenous peoples. In that way he returned to the strategy of violence initiated in 1981.

The Sandinistas are using the same Cessna 337 "push-pull" aircraft to bomb indigenous communities in eastern Nicaragua, as Anastasio Somoza Debayle bombard Ladino communities in western Nicaragua. The

Sandinistas are also using their army against communities that do not support the government, as Somoza did. And travels with the indigenous delegation Robert Martin, a television cameraman who works with ABC. Nicaragua's new national guard also seems determined to catch him, just as Somoza's guard did with another cameraman.

BERNARD Q. NIETSCHMANN Berkeley, California, February 4, 1986. The writer, who is a professor of geography at the University of California, has worked with the Miskito people for 18 years.

Miskito Claims Remain

The Council of Elders of the Nicaraguan Indians announced today that it will take to the International Court of The Hague the demands presented to the government to respect its independence inherited from their ancestors. The foregoing was supported by more than 200 representatives of ethnic groups - churches, Sumos, Blacks and Ramas - who live in the so-called Mosquitia (sic) area, who participated in the General Assembly of the Council. The event that ended the day before in Bluefields, capital of the Autonomous Region of the South Atlantic, sued President Enrique Bolaños, to return the property and rights inherited from their ancestors.

(Prensa Latina cable (Cuba), dated June 30, 2004)

Mosquito Coast Bites Nicaragua's Ortega

A separatist attempt to form a breakaway nation of indigenous people on Nicaragua's jungle shores has the legendary Mosquito Coast buzzing once again — and posing a dilemma for leftist President Daniel Ortega. Frustrated by broken promises of autonomy and generations of exploitation by outsiders, traditional leaders on the rural Atlantic coast are calling for a clean break from Nicaragua and the creation of the Communitarian Nation of the Moskitia (named after the region's indigenous people). On April 19, the indigenous council of elders officially declared the secession of the Atlantic coast from the rest of Nicaragua, warning that if push comes to shove, their independence claims will be backed by a new Indigenous Army of the Moskitia.

"We are not puppets. We are men. And now we have the weight of a nation on our shoulders," said separatist leader Rev. Hector Williams, known as the *Wihta Tara*, or Great Judge of the Nation of Moskitia. The separatist leaders this week declared a state of emergency to protect their lands from the "colonialist" outsiders and sent a letter to U.N. Secretary General Ban Ki-moon asking for support and protection.

Time – May 1, 2009 by Tim Rogers.

The Sandinistas Attack the Miskito Indians--Again

Blog Post *by* Elliott Abrams
September 29, 2015
Council on Foreign Relations

The hostility between the Sandinista regime in Nicaragua and the Miskito Indians of Nicaragua's Atlantic Coast was sharp during the 1980s, and many Indians joined the *contra* effort against that regime. They wanted little more than to be left alone, but the Sandinistas wanted to conscript them into the revolution. To the Marxist Sandinista leaders, they were relics of a pre-capitalist age, and had to brought into 20th century Stalinist reality.

The Sandinistas are back in power in Nicaragua, under the same Daniel Ortega as president, so pity the poor the Indians. Once again they are government targets, and just a week ago 10 were killed. All the old problems about Sandinista interference in Miskito lives is back--but greatly exacerbated now by the canal project. The Sandinistas have enlisted China in a project to build a new trans-Isthmus canal, at a cost of $50 billion. (https://www.cfr.org/blog/sandinistas-attack-miskito-indians-again)

Main Cities and Towns

The Miskito Kingdom consisted and consists of many towns, villages and cities. The most notable are Cabo Gracias a Dios, Sandy Bay, Bluefields and Bilwi. There are also other important cities such as Waspán, Rosita, and Prinzapolka. The first city on our list was the first capital of the Miskito Kingdom, followed by Sandy Bay and Bluefields. Bilwi became important for the timber industry and its port; and later during the rebellion against the Sandinistas.

1. **Cabo Gracias a Dios** (Name given by Christopher Columbus) - Capital of the Kingdom of Moskitia for many decades.

The First Capital of the Miskito Kingdom

2. **Sandy Bay**, the second Miskito capital and residence of many Miskito kings.

3. **Bluefields**, third and last capital of the Kingdom.

Bluefields en el año 1893

4. **Bilwi** – It means snake or snake place in Sumo language. It was renamed Puerto Cabezas, by the Nicaraguan government. Nicaragua brought many "Spaniards" to Nicaraguanize Bilwi. This is why it is a city where Spanish is common. Bilwi as the most important port city of the Moskitia, and was for many decades an important commercial center. At the beginning of the 20th century, Bilwi Timber and Banana Company of New Orleans operated there (later became the Bragman's Bluff Lumber Company), George Emory Company of Boston, and the Standart Fruit Company.

Bilwi has been a rebel Miskito city to the colonialist pretensions of Nicaragua. In the 1980s, it was the main center of rebellion against the Sandinista genocide. Despite the immigration of many Ladinos, the city is clearly and dominantly Miskito.

The Pier of Bilwi
(Built by the Bragman's Bluff Lumber Company, in the 1920s)

CONCLUSION
M K (Miskut Kiamka)

Certainly, there is a lot of information regarding our Miskito nation; both positive and negative. I have focused on the positive aspects of our history given that many of the articles and books that have been written about our nation are contrary to our historical reality and identity. The review presented shows an indomitable people who persist and insist in fighting for their self-determination. Without apology, I must point out that my intention has been to promote Miskito history through the eyes of love for my country.

In the eighties, we lived a period of great suffering because of the genocide that tried to carry out the Sandinista National Liberation Front (FSLN). Our patriotic Miskitos bravely fought to stop them. It is quite possible that their attempt at genocide had to do with revenge. Well, it happens that many Miskitos helped the Marines to catch the supposed hero, Augusto Cesar Sandino. For many Miskitos, Sandino was synonymous of bad news, death and terror. Miskitos of that time reported that when he and his guerrilleros came to the villages, they killed, raped, and took away what little people had. Many Miskitos still remember what he did to the Moravian missionary Bregenzer. I am going to report his murder to have it in context.

Bishop Mueller reports that in 1922, the German missionary Karl Bregenzer went to live in Musawas, among the Sumo (Mayagna) Indians in the Moskitia of Nicaragua, to share with them the Gospel of Christ. He had finished his ministerial studies at the Moravian Theological Seminary in Germany and believed it was

God's will to serve Him in the missions. Brother Bregenzer and his family (wife, two children and mother-in-law) served the Sumo people for many years. But a few years after they arrived, the armed band of Augusto Cesar Sandino emerged. His group used violence against anyone who looked Gringo.

This situation caused the indigenous Miskitos and Sumos to become very worried, because the armed group was reputed to be bloodthirsty. So much so that the Sumos who lived in Musawas and the surrounding villages moved deeper into the mountain, out of fear; fleeing from the Sandinistas. As their pastor, the missionary and his family also went with them, but a short time later they returned. However, a new alarm sounded again, so he sent his family (mother-in-law, wife and two children) back to the mountains with the indigenous people. Although his wife implored him to go with them, he stayed with some indigenous men. He said to his wife with faith: "The Almighty God is still alive" (the one who reported the incident wrote: "The ways of God are mysterious; the mortal cannot understand them").

These were his last words, because "the next day a band of Sandinistas came to the town under the command of the depraved Pedro Blandón". They took the Missionary captive and when he tried to share the Gospel with them or read the New Testament in Spanish, they threw him to the ground violently. On March 31, 1931, the missionary's family read the following text as part of their devotional: "No one has greater love than this that one lay down his life for his friends." That same day the Sandinistas took brother Bregenzer to the corner of the Mission quarters and in cold blood cut off his head with a machete (Mueller 141). The blood of this martyr came to confirm the ancient statement of Tertullian who said: "The blood of the martyrs is the seed of the Church." Today, most Mayagnas believe in Christ; the missionary's death was not in vain.

Me Must Move On

We cannot live or long for the past, but we cannot stop dreaming big, **for a country that was taken from us**. Ours is not a fight of separatism but of repudiation of the colonialism exerted by Nicaragua and Honduras. The knowledge of our history is vital so that we can continue in our fight and work to establish a better future for our children and therefore our Moskitia.

After more than 100 years of occupation, usurpation and exploitation, we must be clear that the governments of Nicaragua and Honduras are not

> After more than 100 years of occupation, usurpation and exploitation, we must be clear that the governments of Nicaragua and Honduras are not interested in Miskito welfare. What's more, it doesn't suit them.

interested in Miskito welfare. What's more, it doesn't suit them. For their conscience tells them that they are occupying other people's land and are surely afraid that one day their legal and moral owners will have enough strength to expel them.

The Moskitia does not exist without the Miskitos. God gave us our land; it belongs to the Moskitia native nations. Historical evidence is in our favor, as is the determination of the Miskito people to want to forge their own destiny. From Miskut to King Robert Henry Clarence, many powers have wanted to occupy our lands. For the moment, Nicaragua and Honduras have succeeded. Both governments have plunged us into economic and educational poverty in order to keep us subjugated. But an ethnic people who have their identity well defined as a nation, can hardly forget their indomitable past. There is no power or human knowledge that can remove that from our Miskito community consciousness.

A nation without economic and educational power can hardly succeed. **That is why it is important that Miskitos who live abroad and have the resources, invest in their Miskito homeland**. It is important that the Miskitos inside and outside teach our children about our history. This book should help in that effort.

We must bear in mind that the mentioned governments have introduced ideas contrary to our ancestral Miskito culture, such as abortion and homosexuality. These actions slowdown the population growth of our people and of course, puts us in enmity with God. We must have to get closer to God. We must leave behind our evil ways. We must reject ideas and traditions that are contrary to our spiritual, social, emotional, cultural and physical well-being. We must reject abortion and homosexuality, which are instruments used by the western governments, academicians, journalists, and Marxist-leftist-progressive groups to reduce and control the multiplication of our people. In addition, they also use vaccines to reduce the fertility of our women.

THIS WE MUST DO

The fight for justice and our autonomy must continue on several fronts. As a nation:

1. *We must turn to God, to the God of Israel.*

¬ We must not allow foreign ideologies to undermine our faith in God and His Word. We have to vigorously reject secularism.

¬ We are to pray for a Moses and leaders that are honest, have integrity and are fearful of God.

2. *Remember our heroes and the historical events of our history with protest, demonstrations, and celebrations; with commemorations and with festivities.*

¬ We must name and rename streets, neighborhoods, educational centers, etc. with the name of our heroes.

3. *Write songs and poems alluding to our Miskito homeland.*

¬ Perform celebratory events and competitions that promote these expressions.

4. *We must have more children and many; the reason why Nicaragua is turning a blind eye with the settlers is to make the number of Miskitos much smaller than that of the Ladinos; as Fallon asserts, the purpose is to have a majority presence using the Ladinos in the Moskitia.*

¬ This means that we cannot accept abortion or homosexuality. For these practices prevent our numerical growth as a nation.

5. *Develop an entrepreneurial attitude and conditions.*

¬ Not to exploit each other, but to promote individual and community well-being.

¬ It is important that within our community consciousness we develop an entrepreneurial mind in order to bring progress to our families. This includes the promotion of education, the development of agriculture, the creation of tourist centers, etc.

6. *We should seek help from international bodies to evict the settlers or people who have acquired land illegally.*

¬ We should not be anti-immigrants but anti-occupation and anti-settlers.

7. *Use our language more frequently and make it richer.*

¬ The use of our language affirms our identity like no other.

¬ The creation of the Miskito Language Academy is key in all this.

We are certainly victims of the occupation, oppression, and injustice of the Nicaraguan government. However, we cannot adopt a victim position, because that is what our victimizers want. To have a victim's spirit is to be a coward, and that leads us to dependence and fear; that does not please God. If we fall into that condition, our victimizers can perpetuate their evil. What we must do is to have faith in God, that He will not let injustice perpetuate.

If the Lord Jesus Christ does not return in the next fifty years, our true autonomy will be completed. I have faith that one of these days God will give us a Moses, a Joshua, a Moshe Dayan, or a Martin Luther King Jr. It is only a matter of time. God is going to raise a man or a woman who fears Him, who is not bribable and seeks the welfare of his or her Miskito people. As we wait for this to happen, we have to fix our faith in God, in the Holy One of Israel and only in Him.

Moihki laikra nani, kaisa wan kupia aiska wal aiwania:

**Yawon pura lubiasa, yawon pura lubiasa
Yu kum, yawon pura lubia sa
Kupi aiskana wal yang lukisna
Yu kum, yawon pura lubia sa. Amen**

APPENDICES

1

Author's General Commentary

This "convention" was led by the Nicaraguan Government with the purpose of creating a "legal" avenue for their occupation and forced annexation of our land to Nicaragua. Historically, the Miskito people has never recognized this convention.

More than 70 "delegates" from the Moskitia who could not read or write - "signed" the so-called "Mosquitia Convention". It has been very well known, by oral tradition, that these delegates were forced by the Nicaraguan soldiers to attend; then they were flattered at Bluefields for several days with large amounts of *guaro* (an alcoholic beverage). In that condition, the Nicaraguan officials had them sign the convention.

- Therefore, this was an illegal convention without moral, ethical and legal validity.
- The Convention was obviously a document aimed to make the Nicaraguan government look good.
- This convention was immoral and illegal, as there was no genuine representation.
- This also applies to the treaties that Nicaragua and Great Britain signed.

"Mosquita (sic) Convention"
November 20, 1894

Considering: that the change verified on February 12 of the current year was due to the effort of the Nicaraguan authority, which wanted to redeem us from the slavery we were in.

Considering: that we have agreed to subject ourselves entirely to the laws and authorities of Nicaragua, to be part of its political and administrative organization.

Whereas: the lack of a respectable and legitimate government is always a cause of calamity for the people, in which case we have been so long.

Considering: that one of the reasons for the backwardness in which we live was undoubtedly that the incomes of the Mosquitia had been defrauded, by investing them in non-administrative purposes.

Whereas: although the Nicaraguan Constitution provides all the needs and aspirations of a free people, we nevertheless wish to retain special privileges that are consistent with our customs and race.

In virtue of all of the above, making use of a natural right and by our free and spontaneous will declare and decree:

Article 1— The Constitution of Nicaragua and its laws shall be obeyed by the mosquito people, these being under the protection of the Republic's flag.

Article 2 - All income produced by the mosquito coast will be invested to its own benefit, thus reserving economic autonomy; but Such income will be collected and managed by the fiscal employees of the Supreme Government.

Article 3 - The indigenous will be exempt in time of peace and war from all military service.

Article 4— No fee will be imposed on the people of the mosquitoes.

Article 5 — The right to vote is extended to men and women aged eighteen.

Article 6 - Indigenous communities shall be immediately subject to the Chief Inspector and mayors and police officers, in their respective locations.

Article 7 - No choice may be made for said employees except in the Indian mosquitoes.

Article 8 - The mayors and police will serve their position for as long as they deserve the trust of the people; but they may be removed by agreement of the Mayor or by popular motion.

Article 9 - When the mayors and police take possession, the Chief Inspector will take them oath using the following formula - "Do you swear by God and the Bible to procure the happiness of the people who have chosen you and obey and enforce the laws of Nicaragua? " The questioner will answer: - "Yes, I swear."

Article 10 - The peoples shall decree their local regulations in Assemblies presided by the Chief, and must submit these regulations to the approval of the superior authority of the National Government on the Coast.

Article 11 - As a vote of gratitude to the Magistrate President of the Republic, General Don J. Santos Zelaya, á, whose efforts are due to us to enjoy freedoms, what was previously called "Mosquito Reserve" from now on will be called "Department of Zelaya."

Given in the Palace of Sessions of the Mosquita Convention, on the twentieth day of the month of November, one thousand eight hundred and ninety-four.

Additional Commentary

Observe the condescending and deceptive language used by the Nicaraguan government in their self-enacted convention. They portray themselves as our liberators when in fact they were becoming our oppressors and occupiers of our land.

- The Miskito people nor the Miskito Kingdom was NEVER under slavery.

- The Miskito people, nor the other inhabitants of the Moskitia agreed to be subjugated by Nicaragua.
- We had a respectable and legitimate King and government, but they were forcefully removed by the Nicaraguan army, through their invasion.
- The income of the Moskitia was not being defrauded; there is no evidence to such claim; in addition, we were happy with our way of life.
- The Nicaraguan constitution did not and does not provide the avenue to seek and achieve our economic prosperity and much less to live in freedom, in our ancestral land.
- The Nicaraguan government did not give us any special privileges; we practice our customs, language and promote our ethnic identity because is our God given right.

Additional Commentary on the Articles

Article 1 – We were and we are forced to obey Nicaraguan laws.

Article 2 – It is well known that Nicaragua has exploited our land and the income from our land has been invested in their country (the pacific and central Nicaragua). That is the reason we are in such backwardness (using their own Convention language) economically, educationally and in infrastructure.

Article 3 – Many Miskitos have been forced to join the Nicaraguan army – the Sandinistas forced our young people to serve in their oppressive forces.

Article 4 – We pay fee and taxes just like the rest.

Article 5 – This so-called right to vote is a joke in Nicaragua – dictatorship and electoral fraud has been the norm in Nicaragua.

Article 6 – Certainly the police, the army and the Nicaraguan officials rule over us.

Article 7 – Historically, the government officers have been Ladinos o Nicaraguans, very few have been Miskitos or from the other ethnic groups.

Article 8 - This article is meaningless since true democracy has never existed in Nicaragua.

Article 9 – This is just lip service.

Article 10 – This is also a worthless declaration.

Article 11 – Jose Santos Zelaya, the then Nicaraguan President and the one who led the invasion to our land, imposed or "called" our land according to his last name. That was another indication of how he viewed our land; as a conquered land.

BIBLIOGRAPHY

Azofeifa Jorge, Ruiz Edward, y Barrantes Ramiro. *Genetic variation and racial admixture in the Miskito of the southern Mosquito Shore, Nicaragua.* Rev. biol. trop vol.46 n.1 San   José Mar. 1998. http://www.scielo.sa.cr/scielo.php?script=sci_a rttext&pid=S0034-77441998000100014. 2/6/2019.

Autonomous   Regions   of   Nicaragua. FADCANIC. Fundación para la Autonomía y el Desarrollo de la Costa Atlántica, n.d. Web. 10 Oct. 2015.

Bataillon, Gilles y Vania Galindo Juárez. *Protestantismo Moravo y Establecimiento de Nuevos Habitus entre Misquitos Nicaragüenses* (1848-2000). Vol. 25, No. 73 (Jan. - Apr., 2007), pp. 41-68 (28 pages) Publicado por: El Colegio de México.

Brooks, David. *US Marines, Miskitos and the Hunt for Sandino: The Rio Coco Patrol in 1928.* Journal of Latin American Studies. Vol. 21, No. 2 (May, 1989), pp. 311-342.

Conzemius Eduard. *Ethnographical survey of the Miskito and Sumu Indians of Honduras and Nicaragua.* 1932. Smithsonian Institution Bureau of American Ethnology. Bulletin 106. Washington, D.C. Print.

Constenla Umaña, Adolfo (1987): "*Elementos de Fonología Comparada de las Lenguas Misumalpa*" Revista de Filología y Lingüística de la Universidad de Costa Rica. 129-161

Cuadra Luciano (tr). *Piratas en Centro América Siglo XVII.* Colección Cultural. Managua, Nicaragua. 1978.

Dampier, William. *A New Voyage Round the World.* 1697. https://quod.lib.umich.edu/e/eebo/A36106.000 1.001/1:6.4?rgn=div2;view=fulltext.web.July 24, 2019.

Dennis, Philip A. (1981). "The Costeños and the Revolution in Nicaragua." *Journal of Interamerican Studies and World Affairs* 23:271-296.

Dennis A. Philip. *Review: The Miskito-Sandinista Conflict in Nicaragua in the 1980s.* Latin American Research Review. Vol. 28, No. 3 (1993), pp. 214-234 (21 pages)

Edson A. Merritt (Capt USMC). *U.S. Marines and Miskito Indians: the Rio Coco patrol of 1928.* USMC, Nicaragua, August 1928. https://mca-marines.org/leatherneck/nicaragua-1928-the-rio-coco-patrol/web.6/01/2018.

Exquemelin, O. Alexandre (John). *The Buccaneers of America; AKA - The Pirates of Panama.* Originally written in Dutch; translated to English in 1684 and published in 1685. Broadway Translations. George Routledge & Sons LTD. London. https://ia802500.us.archive.org/19/items/buccaneersofamer00exquuoft/buccaneersofamer00exquuoft.pdf.web.9/11/19.

Everingham Mark and Taylor Edwin. *Encounters of Moravian Missionaries with Miskitu Autonomy and Land Claims in Nicaragua, 1894 to 1936.* Penn State University Press . *Journal of Moravian History.* No. 7 (Fall 2009), pp. 31-57.

Fagoth Muller, Stedman. *La Mosquitia, Autonomía Regional: Lamento Indigena, Ocaso de una Raza Que se Resiste a Fallecer.* Pub. Unk. 1986.

Fallon, E. Joseph. *A forgotten Country in Central America.* UK Defense Forum. July 25, 2019. https://www.defenceviewpoints.co.uk/articles-and-analysis/a-forgotten-country-in-central-america.web.7/25/2019.

Hale, R. Charles. *Resistance and Contradiction: Miskitu Indians and the Nicaraguan State, 1894-1987.*

Stanford University Press. Stanford, California. 1994.

Helms, Mary W. (1971). *Asang: Adaptations to Culture Contact in a Miskito Community.* Gainesville: University Presses of Florida.

Holm, John Alexander. *The Creole English of Nicaragua's Miskito Coast: its sociolinguistic history and a comparative study of its lexicon and syntax.* Diss. UMI Ann Arbor, 2007.

Journal of Anthropological Research. Vol. 39, No. 2, New World Ethnohistory (Summer, 1983), pp. 198-241 (44 pages). Published by: The University of Chicago Press.

Matamorros, Ruth. *Una Nación más allá de las Fronteras.* WANI. P.29

Muller, A. Karl. *Among Creoles, Miskitos and Sumos.* The Comenius Press. Bethlehem, PA. 1932.

Newson, L. 1987. *Indian Survival in Colonial Nicaragua.* Oklahoma University, Norman and London. 466p.

Nietschmann, Bernard (1973). *Between Land and Water.* New York: Seminar Press.

Nietschmann Bernard. *The Unknown War: The Miskito Nation, Nicaragua, and the United States.* Freedom House, NY. 1989.

Noveck, Daniel. *Class, culture, and the Miskito Indians: a historical perspective.* Dialectical anthropology 13.1 (1988): 17-29.

Olien, Michael D. *The Miskito Kings and the Line of Succession.* Department of Anthropology, University of Georgia, Athens, GA. *Journal of Anthropological Research* 39.2 (1983): 198–241.

Pueblos Indígenas y Tradicionales y Áreas Protegidas - Reserva Biológica Marina de Cayos Miskitos y Franja Costera, Nicaragua. Publicado por UICN, Gland,

Suiza y Cambridge, Reino Unido y WWF International, Gland, Suiza.

Purves, L. David. Ed. *The English Circumnavigators. "The Mosquito Indian of Juan Fernandez"*. Edingburgh. M'Farlane and Erskine. 1874.

Reneouf, W. Robert. *Anglicanismo en Nicaragua* 1745-1985. *Anglican and Episcopal History*. Vol. 57, No. 4 (December 1988), pp. 368-396. Published by: Historical Society of the Episcopal Church.

Rogers, Nicholas. Caribbean Borderland: *Empire, Ethnicity, and the Exotic on the Mosquito Coast.* York University, Toronto. 2002. (*Eighteenth-Century Life*) https://muse.jhu.edu/article/41050/summary. web.7/24/19.

Schaeffer A. Francis. *The Complete Works of Francis A. Schaeffer.* Volume 4. Crossway Books. Westchester, Il. 1982.

Sloane Hans. *A Voyage to the Islands Madera, Barbados, Nieves, S. Christophers and Jamaica. London. 1707. Protocolo Bio-cultural del Pueblo Indígena Miskitu.* Octubre, 2012. http://www.prmapping.res.ku.edu/Protocolo_ Miskitu.pdf.web.7/24/19.

The Awakening Coast: An Anthology of Moravian Writings from Mosquitia and Eastern Nicaragua, 1849-1899. Karl Offen and Terry Rugeley, editors. University of Nebraska Press. Lincoln, Nebraska. 2014.

Vasquez, J. Jorge. *Ruth the Immigrant: An unconventional Interpretation of the Biblical Book of Ruth.* LiderEs. Matthews, NC. 2016.

ABOUT THE AUTHOR

Dr. Jorge J. Vasquez is Miskito, born in Bilwi, Miskito Kingdom. He went into exile in the eighties, due to the genocide and persecution against the Miskitos perpetrated by the government of Nicaragua under the administration of the Sandinistas.

In the United States he gave his life to the Lord Jesus Christ, whom he serves as a preacher, pastor, missionary and teacher. He received his associate degree (AAS) from Forsyth Technical Community College; Bachelor's Degree (BSAS) from Winston Salem State University; MS from St. Thomas University; MMin from Southern Wesleyan University, DMin from John Wesley University (Piedmont International University). He is currently pursuing his PhD in Practical Theology at Logos University.

He is the author of several books:
1. *Homilética Básica*
2. *Hermenéutica Bíblica Básica*
3. *Falsos Maestros, Profetas y Apóstoles: Comentario Exegético de la Epístola de Judas*
4. *Ruth The Immigrant: An Unconventional Interpretation of the Biblical Book of Ruth.*
5. *Rut La Inmigrante: Una Interpretación No Convencional del Libro Bíblico de Rut*
6. *Estilos Prácticos de Evangelismo Personal*
7. *Liderazgo Espiritual: Una Perspectiva Bíblica*
8. *La Educación Bíblica en la Iglesia Local*
9. *Sí Se Puede: Lecciones Prácticas Para el Éxito Personal*

These books are available on Amazon, Barnes and Noble and directly from the author.

Made in the USA
Middletown, DE
22 October 2022

13269694R00073